TULLUS defies death to bring Christ's message to ancient Crete and the fierce Vandals of the North. THE WORD IS HIS SWORD!

TULLUS

fights the myth of THE MINOTAUR stirred up by the cunning Dheka, who plans to use his young captive in a plot to turn Crete against Rome in a bloody, endless war.

TULLUS

confronts natural and man-made disasters—avalanches, mountain mazes, wolves—and VANDALS OF THE NORTH. The Vandals decide that this stranger who speaks of Jesus must be destroyed because his weapon, which promises life, is stronger than any they have ever encountered—and can spell the end of their violent rule!

TULLUS

challenges THE DRAGON SHIP and the Druid priests, who have conspired against this friend of Christ because he is winning their Celtic followers. Captured and facing certain death, Tullus demands trial by ordeal—a right which cannot be denied . . . a rite which no man has ever survived!

TULLUS and the VANDALS OF THE NORTH

David C. Cook Publishing Co.
850 NORTH GROVE AVENUE • ELGIN, IL 60120
In Canada: David C. Cook Publishing (Canada) Ltd., Weston, Ontario M9L 1T4

**TULLUS AND THE VANDALS
OF THE NORTH**
© 1974 David C. Cook Publishing Co.

David C. Cook Publishing Co., Elgin, IL 60120

Printed in the United States of America
Library of Congress Catalog Number: 74-81664

ISBN: 0-912692-44-8

Europe in the First Century

TULLUS
AND THE
MINOTAUR

TULLUS
AND THE MINOTAUR

TULLUS IS A YOUNG CHRISTIAN WHO IS A CITIZEN OF ROME AT THE BEGINNING OF THE CHRISTIAN ERA WHEN IT TOOK REAL COURAGE TO ACCEPT CHRIST AS SAVIOR.

DESPITE THE CRUEL PERSECUTIONS, MORE AND MORE PEOPLE ARE BECOMING CHRISTIANS DUE IN GREAT PART TO THE MISSIONARY WORK OF YOUNG MEN LIKE TULLUS.

THE SHIP ON WHICH TULLUS IS RETURNING TO ROME HAS SAILED BUT A SHORT DISTANCE FROM ALEXANDRIA, EGYPT, WHEN IT RUNS INTO A FIERCE STORM.

THE HURRICANE WINDS DRIVE IT FAR OFF ITS COURSE ONTO SHARP ROCKS WHERE IT IS BATTERED TO PIECES BY THE GIGANTIC WAVES.

THE DISASTER HAPPENS SO QUICKLY THAT TULLUS IS THE ONLY SURVIVOR. DESPERATELY HE CLINGS TO A PIECE OF THE WRECKAGE.

AT DAWN HE IS AROUSED BY THE BUMPING OF HIS TINY RAFT AGAINST THE SHORE. WITH A PRAYER OF THANKSGIVING TO GOD, HE CRAWLS ONTO THE BEACH AND DROPS INTO AN EXHAUSTED SLEEP.

THAT'S NOT A VERY HAPPY CHOICE. I DON'T QUITE UNDERSTAND...

WELL — MOST CRETANS HATE BEING RULED BY ROME AND THIS PARTICULAR PART OF THE COUNTRY IS A HOTBED OF REVOLT...

AND THE ROMANS GRAB ALL THE CHRISTIANS THEY CAN FIND TO SEND TO ROME. I'VE HEARD THEY PUT THEM IN THE ARENA TO BE DEVOURED BY WILD BEASTS.

IF THE CRETAN REBELS FIND YOU, THEY'LL KILL YOU. IF THE ROMANS LEARN YOU'RE A CHRISTIAN, THEY'LL SEND YOU TO THE ARENA. NOW DO YOU UNDERSTAND?

YOU'VE MADE IT VERY CLEAR. HOWEVER, I TRUST GOD TO PROTECT ME FROM BOTH FATES.

I THOUGHT YOU'D SAY THAT. HERE, HAVE SOME OF MY BREAD AND CHEESE. YOU MUST BE HUNGRY. MY NAME'S KASOS. WHAT'S YOURS?

TULLUS. THANKS. I AM HUNGRY.

WHILE TULLUS AND KASOS WERE TALKING, A SINISTER FIGURE SNEAKED UP CLOSE ENOUGH TO OVERHEAR THEM.

I'VE HEARD ENOUGH. MY MASTER WILL PAY ME WELL FOR THIS INFORMATION!

12

AND THE ROMAN GOVERNOR HAS ORDERED YOU TO FIND THE LEADERS OF THE CRETAN REBELS AND TURN THEM OVER TO HIM, OR...

OR HE'LL ENSLAVE ME AND MY FAMILY. WHAT HAS THIS TO DO WITH THE SHIPWRECKED STRANGER?

EVERYTHING! YOU CAN PLACE ALL YOUR TROUBLES ON HIM.

YOU'RE SPEAKING IN RIDDLES.

HEAR ME OUT, MASTER. WITH ALL MY SPYING AND PAYMENTS FOR INFORMATION I HAVEN'T BEEN ABLE TO LEARN WHO THESE LEADERS ARE...

BUT IF WE MAKE THIS YOUNG STRANGER OUT TO BE A GREAT HERO WHO WILL LEAD THE PEOPLE TO THROW OUT THE ROMANS...

THEY'LL FOLLOW HIM AND THE REAL LEADERS WILL BE FORCED TO COME OUT INTO THE OPEN...

AND I COULD GRAB THEM, TURN THEM OVER TO THE ROMANS AND... AH, NO! IT'S TOO CRAZY. WHO WOULD BELIEVE THIS STRANGER WAS A GREAT HERO?

13

THE SUPERSTITIOUS PEOPLE WOULD BELIEVE IF THEY WERE TOLD HE WAS THESEUS RETURNED FROM THE FAR DISTANT PAST!

THESEUS? THE LEGENDARY HERO WHO KILLED THE MINOTAUR?

EXACTLY, MASTER.

"MANY CENTURIES AGO, ACCORDING TO LEGEND, KING MINOS WAS THE RULER OF CRETE. AT KNOSSOS HE BUILT A PALACE WITH A GREAT LABYRINTH OR MAZE SO DEVISED THAT NO ONE ENTERING IT COULD EVER FIND HIS WAY OUT. HERE, KING MINOS KEPT A TERRIBLE MONSTER

—THE MINOTAUR—

A BEAST WITH A BULL'S HEAD ON A HUMAN BODY! EVERY YEAR SEVEN BOYS AND SEVEN GIRLS WERE SACRIFICED TO THIS CREATURE."

THE PEOPLE BLAME YOU FOR ALL THEIR MISERY UNDER THE ROMANS, MASTER.

AND THE ROMANS BLAME ME FOR BEING UNABLE TO FIND THE LEADERS OF THE CRETAN REBELS!

SPREAD THE WORD THAT THIS STRANGER, CAST UP BY THE SEA, IS THE HERO THESEUS. THEN THE REBEL LEADERS WOULD BE FORCED TO COME INTO THE OPEN.

"THESEUS, WITH THE HELP OF KING MINOS' OWN DAUGHTER, ARIADNE, KILLED THE MINOTAUR AND FREED CRETE OF THE TERRIBLE MONSTER."

THE PEOPLE ARE READY TO BELIEVE ANYTHING IF IT MEANS FREEDOM. THEY'LL RALLY BEHIND THIS 'THESEUS' TO A MAN!

IT MIGHT WORK... BUT WHO'S TO SPREAD THE WORD?

THE ORACLE! OF COURSE! THE SUPERSTITIOUS PEOPLE BELIEVE ANYTHING SHE FORETELLS! I'LL GET HER TO PASS THE NEWS!

MEANWHILE, KASOS DRAWS A MAP ON THE SAND FOR TULLUS...

IF YOU'RE DETERMINED TO CONTINUE ON TO ROME RIGHT AWAY, YOUR BEST PLACE TO GET A SHIP IS AT CANDIA, HERE.

THAT'S ALL THE WAY ACROSS THE ISLAND.

YES, AND YOU MUST CROSS THE MOUNTAINS. BUT STAY CLEAR OF KAMARES CAVE ON MOUNT IDA...

WHY?

THAT WAS A HOLY PLACE OF THE ANCIENT MINOANS. THEY SAY A WOMAN ORACLE DWELLS THERE NOW. PEOPLE WHO WANT TO KNOW THE FUTURE GO TO HER. I'VE NEVER BEEN THERE MYSELF. LET'S CLIMB THE CLIFF AND I'LL POINT IT OUT.

THAT'S MOUNT IDA ACROSS THE MESSARA PLAIN THERE, WAIT-- I'LL GO WITH YOU! COME ON, I'LL ASK MY MOTHER AND WE'LL PACK SOME FOOD FOR THE TRIP!

FINE! I HOPE SHE SAYS YES.

16

MOTHER, THIS IS TULLUS. HE'S GOING TO CANDIA TO GET A SHIP FOR ROME AND I WANT TO SHOW HIM THE WAY.

YOU ARE WELCOME TO OUR HUMBLE HOME. COME IN.

THANK YOU.

IT WOULD BE KIND OF YOU TO GUIDE THE YOUNG MAN TO CANDIA. BUT IT IS TOO LATE TO START TODAY. STAY THE NIGHT AND WE'LL DISCUSS IT IN THE MORNING.

I'LL TEND TO MY CHORES, TULLUS. YOU AND MOTHER CAN TALK ABOUT CHRISTIANITY.

A CHRISTIAN! YOU ARE DOUBLY WELCOME. WE CHRISTIANS IN CRETE HAVE FEW CHANCES TO MEET WITH EACH OTHER THESE DAYS!

THE THREE TALK UNTIL LATE INTO THE NIGHT.

I LIKE TO HEAR ABOUT JESUS. BUT IT IS TOO DANGEROUS TO BE A CHRISTIAN NOW.

UNLESS WE CHRISTIANS HAVE THE COURAGE TO STAND UP FOR WHAT WE BELIEVE ALL HOPE FOR THE WORLD WILL BE LOST!

WHILE TULLUS AND HIS NEW FOUND FRIENDS TALK, DHEKA VISITS THE ORACLE IN THE CAVE OF KAMARES...

SO! THE GREAT MAN WHO HAS SOLD HIMSELF TO THE ROMANS SEEKS TO KNOW THE FUTURE! GAZE DEEPLY INTO THE MAGIC SMOKE AND...

ENOUGH! SAVE YOUR SLURS AND MUMBO JUMBO WITCHCRAFT FOR THE FOOLS. I WILL PAY YOU WELL TO DO MY BIDDING. LISTEN CLOSELY...

17

18

19

TULLUS AND KASOS ARE CARRIED DEEP INTO THE KAMARES CAVE AND LEFT THERE, BOUND. DHEKA AND HIS SLAVE GO OFF TO SET THE SCENE FOR TULLUS, AS THESEUS, TO MAKE HIS APPEARANCE.

KASOS! KASOS! ARE YOU ALL RIGHT? DO YOU KNOW WHERE WE ARE?

OOH — MY HEAD! I DON'T KNOW THIS PLACE AT ALL!

HAVE YOU ANY IDEA WHY WE WERE ATTACKED AND LEFT HERE?

NONE AT ALL — I'M SURE THOUGH THAT I RECOGNIZED THAT SLAVE BEFORE I WAS KNOCKED OUT!

HOW ARE WE GOING TO MAKE THE LAD ACT THE PART OF THESEUS, MASTER?

WITH THE BEST PERSUASION IN THE WORLD — THE SORT OF THREATS THAT ALWAYS BRING RESULTS!

KASOS AND HIS MOTHER WILL BE OUR GUARANTEE THAT THIS STRANGER DOES EXACTLY AS WE TELL HIM TO!

BY EVENING, NEWS THAT THE ORACLE WILL MAKE AN IMPORTANT PROPHECY HAS SPREAD FAR AND WIDE... FROM ALL OVER CRETE MEN GATHER AT THE CAVE OF KAMARES TO HEAR HER WORDS.

DRAW NIGH, O MEN OF CRETE, WHO LONG TO THROW OFF THE YOKE OF ROME. LIVE AGAIN IN FREEDOM! I SEE A GREAT HERO FROM THE DISTANT PAST COMING TO LEAD YOU TO VICTORY!

21

THE ORACLE'S WORDS REACH TULLUS AND KASOS WHO ARE SECURELY BOUND WITH ROPES IN THE REAR OF THE CAVE...

LISTEN — A WOMAN'S VOICE! WHAT'S SHE TALKING ABOUT?

I KNOW WHERE WE ARE! THAT'S THE ORACLE'S VOICE. WE'RE IN THE CAVE OF KAMARES!

THERE MUST BE A CROWD LISTENING TO HER — THESEUS — WHAT'S SHE TALKING ABOUT?

I DON'T KNOW BUT I THINK WE'D BETTER GET OUT OF HERE! PRAY TO YOUR GOD FOR HELP. WE CAN NEVER ESCAPE WITHOUT IT!

GO NOW AND ARM YOURSELVES. BE READY WHEN THESEUS APPEARS! YOU WHO HAVE BEEN SECRETLY PLANNING REVOLT MUST NOW MEET WITH THESEUS' VOICE, DHEKA,

SO! THE TRAITOR DHEKA WANTS TO MEET THE REBEL LEADERS! HE MUST HAVE SOME EVIL DESIGN UP HIS SLEEVE.

BUT WHAT'S ALL THIS ABOUT THE HERO, THESEUS, AND WHY ARE WE PRISONERS?

SH-H-H! HERE COMES DHEKA. BE CAREFUL. HE'S BEHIND ALL THIS! I'M SURE!

WELL, WELL! TRUSSED UP LIKE GOATS FOR MARKET! IT'S LUCKY I HAPPENED TO COME THIS WAY. YOU COULD DIE HERE AND NEVER BE DISCOVERED!

LIKE YOU HAVE NEVER DISCOVERED WHO THE REBEL LEADERS ARE?

WATCH YOUR TONGUE, BOY! BOTH YOUR LIVES AND YOUR MOTHER'S TOO, KASOS, DEPEND UPON THIS STRANGER'S COMPLETE OBEDIENCE TO MY WISHES!

22

NOW HEAR ME CAREFULLY. YOU, STRANGER, ARE TO TAKE THE PART OF THESEUS IN A LITTLE SHOW I AM PUTTING ON. YOU WILL KEEP ABSOLUTELY SILENT. I WILL COACH YOU HOW TO ACT AS WE GO ALONG.

DON'T DO IT, TULLUS. THIS MAN CANNOT BE TRUSTED!

I WARN YOU FOR THE LAST TIME, KASOS, KEEP QUIET. YOUR MOTHER IS A PRISONER OF MY SLAVE AT THIS MOMENT. IF ANYTHING GOES WRONG WITH MY PLAN, SHE DIES FIRST.

SAY NO MORE. I WILL DO AS YOU WISH. TRUST IN GOD, KASOS.

WITH THIS FINAL WARNING, DHEKA LEAVES.

WHERE IS YOUR CHRISTIAN GOD, TULLUS? DOES **HE** DESERT **HIS** FOLLOWERS IN A TIME LIKE THIS?

NO, KASOS! GOD NEVER DESERTS **HIS** CHILDREN!

YOU CAN WELL SAY SO — BUT IT'S **MY** MOTHER WHO IS IN DANGER! ONCE THIS EVIL MAN HAS ACCOMPLISHED HIS DESIRE, HE'LL KILL HER. HIS WORD IS WORTHLESS. I DON'T...

PLEASE, KASOS. HAVE FAITH. GOD WILL SAVE US ALL!

AFTER THE ORACLE HAS MADE HER PROPHECY AND HER AUDIENCE HAS LEFT, HER HAND-MAIDENS RUN TO HER...

WE BEG YOU, MISTRESS— DON'T GO ANY FARTHER WITH THIS THESEUS HOAX! IT WILL ONLY BRING TROUBLE TO YOU!

I CAN'T STOP NOW— I HAVE GONE TOO FAR TO TURN BACK.

WELL AT LEAST WE CAN FEED THOSE TWO PRISONERS THAT DHEKA HAS TIED UP IN THE CAVE!

23

24

MARY MAGDALENE?... YOU ARE A CHRISTIAN!

YOU STARTLED ME SO, I NEARLY DROPPED THE FOOD. ARE YOU A CHRISTIAN ALSO?

WELL...NOT EXACTLY. BUT YOUR COMING HERE WITH FOOD MUST BE IN ANSWER TO TULLUS' PRAYERS! I AM BEGINNING TO BELIEVE --- I WANT TO...

THEY TELL THE GIRL THE WHOLE SITUATION...

SO, DHEKA HOLDS YOUR MOTHER! AND AFTER HE HAS USED YOU, TULLUS, FOR HIS THESEUS HOAX, HE WILL SLAY ALL OF YOU! TURN AROUND...

AS A CRETAN I HAVE BEEN FORCED TO SERVE THE ORACLE. BUT I KEEP PRAYING THAT SOMEHOW I CAN HELP MY PEOPLE TO KNOW GOD. PERHAPS THIS IS THE ANSWER TO MY PRAYERS.

COME. I'LL LEAD YOU TO A SECRET WAY OUT OF THE CAVE. BRING THE ROPES SO DHEKA WILL NOT KNOW HOW YOU ESCAPED!

TULLUS, NOW I BELIEVE! GOD DOES ANSWER YOUR PRAYERS!

THE GIRL LEADS THEM FAR BACK INTO THE DEPTHS OF THE CAVE.

CRAWL THROUGH THERE AND YOU'LL BE OUTSIDE. I MUST HURRY BACK BEFORE I'M MISSED. GOD BE WITH YOU!

GOD BLESS YOU FOR WHAT YOU HAVE DONE!

MEANWHILE, AT HIS HOME, DHEKA CONGRATULATES HIMSELF...

THE STUPID REBEL LEADERS WILL STEP FORWARD AS SOON AS MY THESEUS DUPE IS REVEALED. MY SLAVE, BY NOW, HAS KASOS' MOTHER AS A HOSTAGE...

I'LL TELL THE ROMANS THE NAMES OF THE REBELS AND I'LL FORCE THE MOTHER TO TELL ME WHERE THE CHRISTIANS MEET...

THE ROMANS CAN THEN ARREST THE REBELS. I'LL TURN OVER TO THEM ENOUGH CHRISTIANS TO FILL MY QUOTA. I'LL BE WELL REWARDED! AND -AH, YES, I MUST THEN GET RID OF MY SLAVE. HE KNOWS TOO MUCH!

BUT, UNSUSPECTED BY DHEKA, HIS SLAVE HAS IDEAS OF HIS OWN...

DHEKA DOESN'T KNOW THE ROMAN GOVERNOR PAYS ME TO SPY ON MY MASTER! HA—WHAT A REPORT I HAVE TO PASS ON THIS TIME! I CAN FEEL THE WEIGHT OF THE GOLD IN MY POCKET ALREADY!

WHILE KASOS AND TULLUS HURRY TO THE BOY'S HOME BY A BACK TRAIL...

TULLUS, WAIT! THERE'S DHEKA'S SLAVE!

HE'S TALKING TO TWO ROMAN SOLDIERS!

THEY OVERHEAR THE SLAVE TELL THE SOLDIERS THAT DHEKA IS PLOTTING A REVOLT—LEAVING OUT HIS OWN PART IN THE SCHEME. THE SOLDIERS TELL HIM THEY'LL BE READY...

WE'VE HEARD ENOUGH, TULLUS. LET'S HURRY TO MY MOTHER BEFORE THAT DOUBLE-CROSSING SLAVE RETURNS!

WE MUST WARN THE PEOPLE, TOO. THERE'LL BE TERRIBLE BLOODSHED IF THE ROMANS FIND THEM ARMED FOR REVOLT!

MOTHER! ARE YOU ALL RIGHT? YOU HAVEN'T BEEN HURT IN ANY WAY?

PRAISE GOD YOU HAVE RETURNED, KASOS—AND TULLUS, TOO. I PRAYED FOR YOUR SAFETY! I'M ALL RIGHT EXCEPT THESE ROPES ARE SO TIGHT MY ARMS HURT!

THAT BRUTAL SLAVE OF DHEKA'S BURST IN HERE, TIED ME UP AND THEN LEFT. I COULDN'T IMAGINE WHAT WAS GOING ON.

HE'LL BE BACK SOON. BUT WE'LL BE READY FOR HIM.

KASOS' MOTHER SITS WHERE THE SLAVE HAD LEFT HER AS THOUGH STILL BOUND. SOON HE RE-ENTERS THE HUT...

MERCY, MERCY! I WAS ONLY CARRYING OUT MY MASTER'S ORDERS!

WE'LL SHOW YOU THE SAME MERCY YOU WOULD HAVE SHOWN MY MOTHER!

27

TAKING HIS MOTHER TO A FRIEND'S COTTAGE AND LEAVING THE SLAVE SECURELY BOUND IN A GOAT PEN, KASOS HURRIES TULLUS TO THE VILLAGE...

OPEN, OPEN. IT IS KASOS. I HAVE NEWS OF GREAT IMPORTANCE. HURRY-HURRY!

AS SOON AS THE DOOR IS OPENED THEY BURST INSIDE AND TELL THEIR STORY. THEIR TALE IS SO FANTASTIC THAT THEIR LISTENER IS CONFUSED...

IT IS TOO MUCH FOR A POOR MAN LIKE ME TO ACCEPT. COME, TELL IT TO THE LEADERS.

THE REBEL LEADERS LISTEN TO THE STORY OF DHEKA'S EVIL PLOT AND HIS SLAVE'S BETRAYAL

WE KNOW KASOS, BUT THE OTHER IS A ROMAN. CAN WE BELIEVE HIM?

THE ORACLE FORETOLD THE COMING OF THE HERO, THESEUS. SHE IS SACRED, WOULD SHE LIE?

HOW COULD WE EXPLAIN TO THE PEOPLE IF WE ADMITTED WE WERE TAKEN IN BY A HOAX?

THE LEADERS FINALLY COME TO A DECISION...

WE DO NOT LIKE DHEKA OR HIS SLAVE. YET WE CANNOT TAKE YOUR WORD AS THE TRUTH. NOR CAN WE GO AGAINST THE PROPHECY OF THE ORACLE. WE MUST ABIDE BY WHAT FATE HAS IN STORE FOR US!

DISMISSED, TULLUS AND KASOS WONDER WHAT TO DO NOW.

FATE! IT DOESN'T TAKE AN ORACLE TO KNOW THEIR FATE IF THEY GET CAUGHT IN THIS THESEUS PLOT!

WAIT! I HAVE AN IDEA! WE'LL HAVE TO WORK FAST. IN A FEW HOURS THE MOON WILL BE UP! COME ON!

AS THE MOON RISES ABOVE MOUNT IDA, A GREAT CROWD OF CRETAN PEOPLE APPROACH THE CAVE OF KAMARES.

WHILE A LONG FILE OF ROMAN SOLDIERS MARCH SILENTLY FROM THE HILLS TO SURROUND THE OPEN SPACE BEFORE THE CAVE.

THEN THE ORACLE APPEARS...

BOW DOWN, O PEOPLE OF CRETE, THESEUS, WHO HAS RETURNED TO LEAD YOU TO VICTORY OVER YOUR ROMAN OPPRESSORS, IS HERE!

ONE OF THE GIRLS RIPS OFF THE CLOTH--AND WITH A GASP THE CROWD RECOGNIZES **DHEKA!**

THEN, AFTER THEIR FIRST SHOCK, THE PEOPLE BURST INTO ROARS OF LAUGHTER.

DHEKA — THE GREAT HERO DELIVERER!

IMAGINE DHEKA BEING THESEUS!

WHAT'S HE TRYING TO PROVE— THAT HE'S THE WORLD'S GREATEST FOOL?

O HO, HO, HO! ALL THIS BUILD-UP AND WHO APPEARS— DHEKA!

THE ORACLE, AS SURPRISED AS ANYONE, TURNS ON DHEKA IN A FURY...

HOW DARE YOU MAKE A MOCKERY OF ME! I AM RUINED! NO ONE WILL EVER LISTEN TO MY PROPHECIES AGAIN!

AT THAT MOMENT, TULLUS AND KASOS LEAD DHEKA'S SLAVE OUT, BOUND SECURELY. KASOS SHOUTS TO THE CROWD...

NOW LET THE ROMAN TROOPS COME FORWARD WHERE THIS TRAITOR TOLD THEM TO HIDE WHEN HE BETRAYED BOTH YOU AND HIS MASTER!

31

THE SOLDIERS LET THE PEOPLE RETURN TO THEIR HOMES. BUT DHEKA AND HIS SLAVE ARE TAKEN TO THE GOVERNOR.

THE GOVERNOR WILL LIKE TO QUESTION THESE TWO.

WHEN THE VILLAGERS ASK TULLUS AND KASOS HOW THEY MANAGED THE TRICK, KASOS EXPLAINS...

THE TREACHERY HAD TO BE EXPOSED IN FRONT OF YOU AND THE ROMAN TROOPS. WE HAD THE SLAVE. IT WAS EASY FOR THE TWO BRAVE GIRLS TO LURE DHEKA TO THE CAVE WHERE WE OVERPOWERED HIM.

THEN TULLUS SPEAKS...

AND MAY THIS BE A LESSON—DO NOT PUT YOUR TRUST IN FALSE PROPHETS OR RELY UPON WEAPONS TO SOLVE YOUR PROBLEMS. TURN TO GOD AND FIND YOUR PEACE AND HAPPINESS IN THE TEACHINGS OF CHRIST!

HE IS A CHRISTIAN!

AYE. WE SHOULD LEARN MORE OF CHRIST.

ON THE WAY BACK TO KASOS' HOME TULLUS AND KASOS MEET THE TWO HANDMAIDENS OF THE ORACLE.

PRAISE GOD—THE ORACLE HAS TURNED US LOOSE!

COME TO MY MOTHER'S HOME AND REST BEFORE YOU START.

NOW WE CAN GO BACK TO OUR HOMES.

KASOS' MOTHER WELCOMES THE TWO GIRLS. AFTER A FEW DAYS ONE OF THE TWO GIRLS RETURNS TO HER VILLAGE ON THE OTHER SIDE OF CRETE. BUT KASOS AND THE GIRL WHO HAD GIVEN THEM FOOD IN THE CAVE DECIDE TO MARRY AND STAY WITH KASOS' MOTHER.

IN THE MEANTIME TULLUS PREACHES THE WORD OF GOD TO THE PEOPLE IN THE VILLAGES. THEY NEVER HEAR OF DHEKA AND HIS SLAVE AGAIN.

THEN, TULLUS AGAIN BOARDS A SHIP FOR ROME LEAVING A HAPPY GROUP OF FRIENDS AND MANY CONVERTS TO CHRISTIANITY.

THE END.

TULLUS
and the
VANDALS
OF THE NORTH

TULLUS and the VANDALS OF THE NORTH

HIGH ON A CRAG IN THE ALPS MOUNTAINS AN IBEX STUDIES THE LONE FIGURE OF A MAN TOILING ALONG THE ROMAN MILITARY ROAD THAT WINDS UPWARD FROM THE VALLEY FAR BELOW.

THE LONE FIGURE IS TULLUS, WHO IS ON HIS WAY NOW TO PREACH THE GOSPEL AS JESUS TOLD HIS FOLLOWERS TO DO IN MARK 16:15.

HE IS HEADING NORTH OF THE DANUBE RIVER TO THE COUNTRY OF THE VANDALS.

AS DARKNESS BEGINS TO FALL, TULLUS COMES TO A SMALL HOSTEL BESIDE THE TRAIL.

HO, LANDLORD! OPEN UP FOR A HUNGRY, WEARY TRAVELER!

COMING, COMING! NO NEED TO KNOCK DOWN THE DOOR!

IF YE CAN PAY FOR YOUR FOOD AN' A NIGHT'S LODGING, YE MAY ENTER! ELSE YE CAN BE ON YOUR WAY OR SLEEP OUTSIDE WITH THAT EMPTY-PURSE CLOWN THERE!

A FIGURE THAT TULLUS HAD NOT NOTICED RISES FROM A PILE OF HAY IN THE COURTYARD.

CLOWN INDEED! A SINGER OF HERO'S DEEDS AM I. AT THE MOMENT OUT OF FUNDS 'TIS TRUE, BUT WILLING TO PAY WITH MERRY TUNES WORTH MORE THAN GOLD!

BAH! CAN I PAY THE TAX COLLECTOR WITH MERRY TUNES? OR FOR THE BREAD AND MEAT YOU WOULD GOBBLE?

36

Panel 1:

HOLD, LANDLORD. A FEW SONGS WILL HELP PASS THE EVENING PLEASANTLY. COME, FRIEND, BE MY GUEST!

INVITE WHOM YE PLEASE. AS LONG AS YE PAY IN ADVANCE.

AH, SIR, YOUR KINDNESS WILL BE WELL REWARDED.

Panel 2:

AFTER A HEARTY MEAL THE YOUNG FELLOW ENTERTAINS TULLUS WITH SONGS AND LIVELY TUNES ON HIS HARP. EVEN THE GROUCHY LANDLORD IS FORCED TO NOD HIS HEAD AND TAP HIS FOOT TO THE RHYTHM.

Panel 3:

EARLY NEXT MORNING TULLUS STARTS OFF. HIS NEW FRIEND DECIDES TO GO WITH HIM AND CHATTERS AWAY WITHOUT GIVING TULLUS TIME TO GET IN A WORD.

MY MOTHER NAMED ME ORPHEUS. SHE WAS GREEK AND LOVED MUSIC. WHEN BOTH MY PARENTS DIED I CAME TO ROME TO MAKE MY FORTUNE. BUT WITH THAT CRAZY EMPEROR GIVING FREE CIRCUSES NO ONE WILL PAY TO HEAR A POOR SINGER.

Panel 4:

NOW I'M GOING TO TRY MY LUCK AMONG THE TROOPS GUARDING THE BORDER. I'VE HEARD THEY PAY WELL FOR ENTERTAINMENT. THEIR DUTY IS SO MONOTONOUS!

Panel 5:

YOU DON'T TALK MUCH DO YOU? WHY DON'T YOU TELL ME ABOUT YOURSELF?

YOU HAVEN'T GIVEN ME A CHANCE. I...LISTEN... WHAT'S THAT RUMBLING NOISE ABOVE US?

IT'S THE GOD OF THE MOUNTAIN! HE'S GOING TO SLAY US FOR NOT MAKING A SACRIFICE TO HIM THIS MORNING!

THERE IS BUT ONE GOD AND HE DOES NOT SLAY!

ALL GODS SLAY THOSE WHO DISPLEASE THEM! WE ARE LOST!

NOT YET. I SEE A PLACE OF SAFETY!

TULLUS RACES UP THE ROAD URGING HIS FRIEND ALONG. HERE ROMAN ENGINEERS HAVE CUT THE ROAD INTO THE STEEP CLIFF LEAVING AN OVERHANG COVERING THE TRAIL.

IS YOUR GOD MORE POWERFUL THAN THIS GOD OF THE MOUNTAIN?

HE IS ALL-POWERFUL BECAUSE HE'S THE ONLY TRUE GOD. TRUST IN HIM!

JUST AS TULLUS SAYS THIS THE AVALANCHE THUNDERS DOWN. ALTHOUGH THE OVER-HANGING CLIFF SHAKES WITH THE WEIGHT OF SNOW AND ROCKS, IT HOLDS, AND THE MIGHTY MASS ROARS OVER AND DOWN TO THE VALLEY BELOW.

THANKFUL FOR THEIR NARROW ESCAPE THEY CHEERFULLY START OFF AGAIN. BUT AS THEY TURN A BEND IN THE TWISTING ROAD...

THE ROAD'S BLOCKED! WHAT'LL WE DO?

WE CAN'T CROSS OVER ON THAT LOOSE SNOW. WE'LL HAVE TO CLIMB AROUND IT.

HOW MUCH FARTHER, TULLUS?

CAN'T BE MUCH. WE'VE BEEN CLIMBING FOR A LONG TIME.

A BEAUTIFUL VIEW, BUT WHERE'S THE ROAD?

OVER THERE? NO—MUST BE THAT WAY—OR...

WE'RE REALLY LOST NOW! AND IT'S GETTING DARK!

I—I GUESS WE'LL HAVE TO SPEND THE NIGHT UP HERE AND WAIT FOR DAYLIGHT!

THEY FIND A SHELTERED SPOT AND PREPARE TO SIT OUT THE COLD NIGHT UNAWARE THAT FIERCE EYES ARE GLARING DOWN AT THEM.

40

41

SUDDENLY THE STILLNESS OF THE NIGHT IS SHATTERED BY THE BLOODCURLING HOWLS OF A WOLF PACK!

TULLUS! DO YOU HEAR THAT?

WOLVES!

WE HAVE NO WEAPONS, NO FIRE... NOTHING TO WARD THEM OFF!

YES WE HAVE—GET OUT YOUR HARP.

THE WOLF PACK RACES TOWARD THEM. JUST AS THEY GET CLOSE, ORPHEUS TWANGS LOUDLY ON HIS HARP, SINGING A LIVELY SONG WITH TULLUS JOINING IN.

THE UNUSUAL SOUND STOPS THE WOLVES IN THEIR TRACKS! THEIR EARS TWITCH FORWARD...

THEY LOOK JUST LIKE MUSIC CRITICS I'VE PLAYED FOR!

DON'T BREAK THE SPELL—KEEP SINGING!

42

SLOWLY THEY WALK TOWARD THE WOLF PACK SINGING AND SHOUTING AND TWANGING THE HARP. THE WOLVES BACK AWAY AS THEY APPROACH. ON AND ON THEY MARCH GRADUALLY INCREASING THEIR PACE.

FINALLY THE WOLVES MELT INTO THE PITCH BLACK DARKNESS AND DISAPPEAR. TULLUS AND ORPHEUS KEEP GOING—SUDDENLY THEY TUMBLE OVER THE EDGE OF A CLIFF! UNABLE TO CHECK THEMSELVES THEY PLUNGE DOWN ITS STEEP ICE-ENCRUSTED SLOPE.

44

NOT FAR AWAY, A SQUAD OF SOLDIERS ARE WORKING THROUGH THE NIGHT CLEARING THE MILITARY ROAD BLOCKED BY SNOW FROM THE RECENT AVALANCHE.

SOMETHING JUST FELL OFF THAT CLIFF AND I THOUGHT I HEARD A YELL!

SO DID I. LET'S TAKE A LOOK!

A HARP! LYING ON THE SNOW. COULD AN ANGEL HAVE DROPPED IT?

HO! YOU MEN BRING YOUR SHOVELS AND TORCHES!

DIG CAREFULLY, MEN, THERE MAY BE SOMEONE BURIED UNDER THE SNOW.

IT'S A MAN—A TRAVELING MINSTREL AT THAT!

ALL RIGHT, MEN. BACK TO CLEARING THE ROAD!

NO! NO! DIG FURTHER. MY FRIEND IS ALSO BURIED HERE.

TULLUS IS QUICKLY UNCOVERED AND HAULED OUT OF THE DEEP SNOWDRIFT.

YOU CAN THANK THE GODS FOR YOUR ESCAPE.

I THANK YOU FOR DIGGING US OUT AND I THANK THE ONE GOD FOR ANSWERING MY PRAYERS THAT GUIDED YOU TO US.

MY HARP WAS NOT DAMAGED!

YOU SOUND LIKE A CHRISTIAN!

46

A WEEK LATER AND MANY MILES FURTHER ON THEIR JOURNEY—THEY COME UPON A STRANGE SCENE...

JUST AS TULLUS AND ORPHEUS RUN UP TO THE THREE PEOPLE WHO ARE STRUGGLING THE YOUNGER MAN THROWS THE GIRL AND THE OLDER MAN TO THE GROUND...

DON'T TAKE HIM—DON'T, I BEG YOU!

SEEING TULLUS AND ORPHEUS, HE RUNS OFF, DISAPPEARING INTO THE FOREST.

HE WAS GOING TO STEAL BORAN. YOU SCARED HIM OFF!

YOU MEAN HE WAS GOING TO KIDNAP THAT MAN?

NO, NO! THAT IS MY FATHER.

HE WANTED BORAN, OUR DANCING BEAR!

WE ARE TRAVELING ENTERTAINERS. THIS IS MY DAUGHTER, LANI.

HO! ORPHEUS, HERE ARE COMPANIONS FOR YOU—EVEN THE BEAR!

48

That man followed us from the last village. He wanted to get Boran and make a robe for himself from Boran's fur!

He's too cowardly to hunt a wild bear! Boran wouldn't hurt anyone and he knew it!

But alas, I am too old to protect Lani or Boran any longer. If you hadn't come along he would have taken Boran and probably Lani, too!

Since both parties are going north they decide to travel together.

I play the flute while Boran dances. You have a harp. Perhaps you will play with us!

What? **Me** play for a dancing bear?

Really! The very thought is sickening!

Ho, your daughter and Orpheus seem to have disagreed about something!

It probably has to do with Boran. She loves him!

At each village they put on a show. Orpheus sings and plays his harp. Then Lani plays the flute while Boran dances. Tullus talks about Jesus and his promise of salvation to those who will listen.

You must admit she draws a bigger audience than either you or I do!

Pooh! A dancing bear is about all these peasants understand.

49

UNTIL NEARLY DAWN TULLUS PRAYS TO GOD FOR GUIDANCE.

HELP ME, O, LORD, TO TELL THESE PEOPLE CHRIST'S WONDERFUL MESSAGE SO THEY WILL LISTEN AND KNOW THE TRUTH!

NEXT DAY AS THEY CONTINUE THEIR JOURNEY, ORPHEUS WALKS AHEAD WITH LANI.

WHEN WE COME TO THE NEXT VILLAGE, LANI, WOULD YOU LET TULLUS ENTER ALONE AND SPEAK TO THE PEOPLE BEFORE...

BEFORE MY PRECIOUS BORAN DANCES AND OUTSHINES HIS TALK AND YOUR SINGING? YOU'RE BOTH JEALOUS OF HIM!

THAT WAS UNFAIR, LANI, AND YOU KNOW IT. TULLUS IS DEDICATED TO HIS GOD. ALL HE WANTS IS TO EXPLAIN TO THE PEOPLE WITHOUT THE DISTRACTION OF A DANCING BEAR!

AND I SUPPOSE YOU WISH TO SING BEFORE YOUR AUDIENCE IS ALSO DISTRACTED BY BORAN'S DANCING?

VERY WELL. MY FATHER AND I WILL KEEP BORAN IN THE FOREST. YOU AND TULLUS CAN GO INTO THE VILLAGE. NO ONE WILL LISTEN TO EITHER OF YOU. YOU'LL SEE!

BUT WHEN THEY REACH THE NEXT VILLAGE...

THE VILLAGE HAS BEEN BURNED!

IT'S STILL SMOLDERING!

VANDALS! WE MUST BE CLOSE TO THE BORDER!

SUDDENLY THEY COME UP TO THE SURVIVORS OF THE RAID, SEARCHING THE RUINS FOR ANYTHING OF VALUE...

LOOK! LOOK! OUR TOTEM* COMES TO REVENGE US!

*A TOTEM TO PRIMITIVE PEOPLE WAS A SYMBOL OF THEIR CLAN AND THEIR GOD.

BEFORE TULLUS OR THE OTHERS CAN STOP THEM, A GROUP OF MEN RUSH UP, GRAB THE BEAR, AND DRAG HIM AWAY!

WE WILL REBUILD OUR VILLAGE AND HE WILL PROTECT IT!

THE ROMANS CANNOT PROTECT US, BUT NOW—WE ARE SAFE!

HE IS THE SPIRIT OF OUR ANCESTORS!

IN VAIN LANI TRIES TO REACH HER BEAR...

GIVE HIM BACK TO ME! HE IS NO GOD—HE IS MINE! I RAISED HIM FROM A CUB!

SILENCE, WOMAN! THE BEAST IS YOURS NO LONGER. NO WOMAN MAY TOUCH A BEAR—HE IS SACRED TO US. YOU WILL NOT BE SLAIN ONLY BECAUSE YOU LED HIM TO US.

WHILE THE FOUR TRAVELERS LOOK ON HELPLESSLY, BORAN IS LED OFF INTO THE WOODS. THE VILLAGERS STOP SEARCHING THE RUINS TO FOLLOW. LANI TURNS ANGRILY TO TULLUS...

I SUPPOSE YOU AND YOUR HARP-PLAYING FRIEND ARE HAPPY NOW THAT MY BORAN IS LOST TO ME!

NO, LANI. WE FEEL AS BADLY AS YOU. THIS HAPPENED SO SUDDENLY WE HAD NO CHANCE TO INTERFERE!

HOW WILL WE LIVE WITHOUT THE FEW COINS HIS CLEVER DANCING BROUGHT US?

TULLUS AND I WILL TAKE CARE OF YOU AND YOUR FATHER. PLEASE DON'T CRY.

WITH GOD'S HELP I'LL GET BORAN BACK. YOU ALL WAIT HERE.

FEARFUL THAT THE POOR BEAST MIGHT BE SACRIFICED, TULLUS FOLLOWS THE VILLAGERS INTO THE WOODS, TELLING THE OTHERS TO WAIT FOR HIS RETURN.

THE PATH LEADS HIM TO A SMALL CLEARING...

O GOD! HELP ME TURN THESE PEOPLE FROM THEIR PAGAN BELIEFS TO YOU!

53

PUSHING THROUGH THE RING OF WILDLY DANCING AND YELLING MEN, TULLUS SHOUTS LOUDLY...

STOP! STOP!

THIS DUMB BEAST IS NOT THE SPIRIT OF ANY GOD. HIS SACRIFICE WILL NOT HELP YOU. LISTEN AND I WILL TELL YOU OF THE TRUE GOD IN WHOM YOU CAN TRUST!

FOR A MOMENT THE PEOPLE ARE SHOCKED TO SILENCE BY THIS INTERRUPTION. THEN THOSE THAT HAD BEEN DANCING AROUND THE BEAR ANGRILY CLOSE IN ON TULLUS...

WHO DARES BREAK INTO THE HOLY CIRCLE?

DEATH TO THE STRANGER!

BUT BEFORE THEY TOUCH HIM SOME WOMEN ONLOOKERS SHRIEK AT THEM...

LET HIM SPEAK! LET HIM SPEAK!

WE WANT TO HEAR ABOUT A GOD THAT CAN BE TRUSTED!

THE OLD GODS HAVE NEVER PROTECTED US FROM VANDAL RAIDS. WE SACRIFICE TO THEM BUT THEY DO NOT HELP WHEN WE NEED THEM!

IF THERE IS A TRUER GOD WE WANT TO KNOW ABOUT HIM!

SPEAK, STRANGER! TELL US HOW WE MAY LIVE WITHOUT FEAR!

QUICKLY TAKING ADVANTAGE OF THE HUSH THAT FOLLOWS THE WOMEN'S DEMANDS, TULLUS TELLS THEM ABOUT CHRIST AND HIS LOVE FOR THEM.

HE URGES THEM TO GIVE UP THEIR WORSHIP OF FALSE GODS AND TURN TO CHRIST.

HE TELLS OF JESUS' PROMISE OF SALVATION FOR THOSE WHO REALLY ACCEPT HIM.

WHEN HE IS FINISHED THE CROWD GOES BACK TO THEIR RUINED VILLAGE DISCUSSING HIS MESSAGE AMONG THEM- SELVES.

BUT ONE NATIVE HIDES BEHIND A TREE AND WATCHES TULLUS UNFASTEN THE NEARLY STRANGLED BEAR TO LEAD HIM BACK TO HIS MISTRESS...

HE FREED THE BEAST AND THE GODS DID NOT INTERFERE!

THE REUNION BETWEEN LANI AND HER BELOVED PET IS A JOYFUL OCCASION...

YOU HAVE MADE MY DAUGHTER MOST HAPPY, TULLUS!

I AM MOST HAPPY THAT THOSE PEOPLE LISTENED TO ME!

I'D BE HAPPY IF LANI WERE AS HAPPY TO SEE ME!

THAT NIGHT, THE STRANGER WHO HAD LISTENED TO TULLUS FROM BEHIND A TREE, PADDLES ACROSS THE WIDE RIVER IN HIS HIDE-COVERED BOAT.

I MUST REPORT WHAT I SAW AND HEARD TO THE CHIEFS!

DAWN IS JUST BREAKING AS HE STEPS ASHORE AND IS CHALLENGED BY A SENTRY...

HO! KEEP YOUR HANDS HIGH IN THE AIR!

LOWER YOUR SPEAR, IT IS I, GERTH. I HAVE GREAT NEWS TO TELL!

HEARING THE SENTRY'S CHALLENGE, THE CHIEFS RUSH TO THE SHORE.

GERTH! WHAT NEWS DO YOU BRING?

HAVE THE ROMANS LEFT THEIR FORT TO AVENGE OUR RAID ON THE VILLAGE?

I HAVE A STRANGE STORY TO TELL!

I OVERHEARD A STRANGER, A ROMAN BY HIS SPEECH, TELL THE SURVIVORS OF THE VILLAGE THAT ROME IS NO MORE—A NEW KINGDOM IS AT HAND!

THE STRANGER SPOKE OF A NEW POWERFUL GOD THAT HAS DESTROYED ALL OTHER GODS. THEN HE TOOK AWAY THE BEAR THAT WAS TO BE SACRIFICED, AND NOTHING HAPPENED TO HIM!

HE DARED TO STOP A SACRIFICE?

HO! THE OLD GODS MUST SURELY BE REPLACED!

THE PRIEST SPEAKS...

IF THIS IS TRUE LET US TAKE ADVANTAGE OF IT, BUT I DO NOT LIKE THIS TALK OF A NEW GOD.

OUR GODS HAVE BROUGHT US VICTORY OVER THE ROMANS AND PREVENTED THEIR LEGIONS FROM INVADING OUR LANDS ON THIS SIDE OF THE RIVER!

THIS MAN MUST BE TALKING ABOUT OUR ALL-POWERFUL GOD AND FORETELLING OUR CONQUEST OF ROME!

THE VANDAL SPY HAS ENTIRELY MISUNDERSTOOD THE MESSAGE TULLUS HAD SPOKEN OF TO THE VILLAGERS ACROSS THE RIVER.

TULLUS WAS SPEAKING OF GOD'S KINGDOM AND OF CHRIST'S PROMISE TO THOSE WHO WOULD FOLLOW HIM.

THEN THE HEAD CHIEF OF THE VANDALS SPEAKS...

THERE IS ONLY ONE WAY TO FIND OUT THE TRUTH OF THIS STRANGER'S TALE. BRING HIM HERE AND WE'LL PUT HIM TO THE TEST! IF IT IS BUT A ROMAN TRICK TO PUT US OFF GUARD WE'LL QUICKLY FIND OUT!

MEANWHILE, TULLUS AND HIS FRIENDS HAVE TRAVELED ON TO THE ROMAN FORT GUARDING THE FRONTIER.

YOU BROUGHT NEW HOPE TO THOSE VILLAGERS, TULLUS. I, TOO, NOW BELIEVE IN JESUS.

I AM GLAD, WARTH.

I WONDER WHAT AWAITS US HERE, ORPHEUS.

WHATEVER IT IS, LANI, I HOPE WE'LL SHARE IT TOGETHER.

WHILE HIS COMPANIONS ENTERTAIN THE TROOPS, TULLUS TALKS WITH THE COMMANDER.

I CANNOT GIVE YOU PERMISSION TO CROSS THE RIVER INTO VANDAL COUNTRY.

BUT I MUST GO THERE, SIR!

MANY WISH TO CROSS OVER AND TRADE WITH THEM. BUT WE ARE HANGING ON HERE BY THE SKIN OF OUR TEETH. I COULD NOT GUARANTEE YOUR SAFETY—I CAN'T GUARANTEE IT EVEN ON THIS SIDE. THE VANDALS CROSS OVER AT WILL!

THAT EVENING TULLUS WALKS ALONE BESIDE THE RIVER PRAYING GOD TO HELP HIM BRING CHRIST'S WORDS TO THE VANDALS. BEFORE HIM, HIDDEN IN THE REEDS, TWO OF THE VANDALS LIE IN WAIT...

SILENTLY THEY APPROACH HIM . . .

HA — I HAVE NEVER MADE A BETTER CAST WITH A NET!

NOR CAUGHT A MORE WANTED BIRD!

REALIZING THESE ARE VANDALS TULLUS MAKES NO OUTCRY—IT'S AN UNCOMFORTABLE AND AN UNDIGNIFIED WAY, BUT HE'LL GET INTO VANDAL COUNTRY WITHOUT DISOBEYING THE ROMAN COMMANDER.

THEY ARE MET ON THE OTHER SIDE BY A GROUP OF VANDAL WARRIORS WAITING TO ESCORT TULLUS TO THEIR VILLAGE.

NEXT MORNING HE IS LED BEFORE THE CHIEF...

GERTH, THE VANDAL SPY, ACTS AS INTERPRETER BETWEEN TULLUS AND THE VANDALS.

THE CHIEF WANTS TO HEAR MORE ABOUT THIS KINGDOM YOU SPEAK OF.

I'LL GLADLY TELL HIM OF GOD'S KINGDOM!

MEANWHILE, ORPHELIS SEARCHES ALL OVER THE ROMAN FORT FOR TULLUS.

I CANNOT FIND TULLUS ANYWHERE, LANI. SURELY HE WOULDN'T HAVE CROSSED THE RIVER DURING THE NIGHT WITHOUT TELLING US FIRST!

COULD THE ROMANS HAVE IMPRISONED HIM TO PREVENT HIS GOING? I KNOW THE COMMANDER FORBADE HIM.

IF THEY HAVE THEY WON'T ADMIT IT.

ORPHEUS AND LANI CONFRONT THE ROMAN COMMANDER.

WHAT? HE'S MISSING AND YOU ACCUSE ME OF HIDING HIM?

WE'RE NOT ACCUSING YOU, SIR. WE'RE ASKING IF YOU KNOW HIS WHEREABOUTS.

I DON'T KNOW. BUT IF HE HAS CROSSED OVER INTO VANDAL COUNTRY AGAINST MY ORDERS I'LL HAVE HIM SENT BACK TO ROME IN CHAINS IF HE RETURNS HERE! AND THAT GOES FOR YOU, TOO, IF YOU BOTHER ME AGAIN!

IT'S NOT LIKE TULLUS TO RUN OFF WITHOUT TELLING YOU OF HIS PLANS.

YOU'RE RIGHT. I THINK YOU AND YOUR FATHER SHOULD GO BACK TO THAT VILLAGE WHERE TULLUS PREACHED. WAIT THERE UNTIL YOU HEAR FROM ME.

WHILE ACROSS THE RIVER, TULLUS EXPLAINS THE KINGDOM OF GOD TO THE CHIEF AND A GROUP OF VANDAL WARRIORS.

NOT SO FAST. I HAVE TO TRANSLATE YOUR WORDS.

FOR HOURS THE VANDALS LISTEN INTENTLY. THEN SUDDENLY THE CHIEF AND HIS WARRIORS LEAP TO THEIR FEET SHOUTING AND BRANDISHING THEIR WEAPONS!

WHAT DID YOU TELL THEM I SAID?

JUST WHAT YOU TOLD ME TO...AS NEARLY AS I COULD TRANSLATE IT...THAT THOSE WHO FOLLOW YOU WILL NEVER DIE AND THAT A GREAT HOST WILL JOIN US AND DESTROY ROME AND...

ENOUGH! ENOUGH! O, DEAR GOD, WHAT HAVE I DONE?

I TRIED TO TELL THEM ABOUT JESUS LEADING THEM—ABOUT EVERLASTING LIFE—THAT GOD WILL DESTROY EVIL. BUT THEY HAVE COMPLETELY MISUNDERSTOOD MY WORDS!

AND WHILE THE WARRIORS DANCE AROUND THE CAMPFIRE IN A FRENZY OF WILD CELEBRATION, TULLUS SITS APART...

O, GOD, SHOW ME HOW I CAN UNDO THE HARM I HAVE DONE!

THE CELEBRATION GOES ON AND ON. TULLUS SADLY RETURNS TO HIS HUT. SUDDENLY...

PSS—T, TULLUS! I KNEW I'D FIND YOU!

ORPHEUS! HOW DID YOU GET HERE?

SWAM, OF COURSE. WE GREEKS ARE HALF FISH YOU KNOW. THESE VANDALS ARE SO BUSY YELLING AND DANCING THE WHOLE ROMAN ARMY COULD HAVE CROSSED THE RIVER UNDETECTED!

YOU SHOULDN'T HAVE TAKEN SUCH A CHANCE ALTHOUGH I'M GLAD YOU DID. I'M IN A TERRIBLE FIX!

63

BUT GERTH, THE ONLY VANDAL WHO CAN TRANSLATE THE LANGUAGES HAS HIS OWN IDEAS...

YOU WERE RIGHT. THE STRANGER IS HERE TO MAKE SURE WE ARE READY FOR THE WAR AND HE SAYS YOU SHALL BE THE KING WHEN WE REACH ROME!

HA! THE KING! IT IS GOOD. TELL HIM WE ARE READY!

HE TELLS TULLUS AND ORPHEUS...

THE KING—ER, CHIEF WELCOMES YOU, STRANGER. HE ASSURES YOU THAT WE ARE NOT PREPARING FOR WAR. WE ARE MERELY CHECKING OUR ARMS. HE IS DEEPLY INTERESTED IN YOUR RELIGION, TOO.

I DON'T LIKE TO THINK EVIL OF A MAN, ORPHEUS, BUT I HAVE A FEELING GERTH IS NOT TRUTHFUL!

SO YOU NOTICED THAT SLIP OF HIS TONGUE! I DON'T KNOW WHY, BUT I'M SURE HE'S NOT TELLING THE CHIEF WHAT WE ARE SAYING!

PSST—I GO TO THE FOREST. FOLLOW, BUT LET NO ONE SUSPECT.

SHE SPEAKS OUR TONGUE!

SH—ORPHEUS. GERTH MAY BE WATCHING!

THE GUARD AT THE GATE SALUTES WITH HIS SPEAR AND LETS THEM PASS WITHOUT QUESTION.

THEY REACH THE FOREST...

THERE SHE IS. I WONDER WHAT SHE WANTS WITH US?

WE'LL SOON FIND OUT.

64

65

MEANWHILE, LANI AND HER FATHER HAVE LEFT THE ROMAN FORT AND GONE BACK TO THE FRIENDLY VILLAGE WITH THEIR DANCING BEAR.

LOOK! LOOK! THE BEAR HAS RETURNED!

NOW WE'LL HAVE SOME FUN!

WELCOME BACK. BUT WHERE IS THE HARP PLAYER AND THE ONE WHO SPOKE OF HIS GOD?

ALAS, WE KNOW NOT. BOTH HAVE DISAPPEARED INTO VANDAL COUNTRY.

HM-M, THAT IS BAD. THERE ARE RUMORS THAT THE VANDALS ARE PREPARING FOR WAR!

ONE OF THE VANDALS, HIS NAME IS GERTH, IS DUE TO BRING SOME AMBER ACROSS THE RIVER TONIGHT. HE CAN'T TRADE WITH THE ROMANS DIRECTLY SO HE DEALS THROUGH US. I'LL ASK HIM FOR NEWS.

WHILE TULLUS AND ORPHEUS WALK FARTHER INTO THE FOREST, EACH IS DEEP IN THOUGHT. FINALLY TULLUS BREAKS THE SILENCE...

I THINK GOD HAS GIVEN ME THE ANSWER, ORPHEUS.

GOOD. MY MIND'S BEEN A TOTAL BLANK. LET'S HEAR YOUR PLAN.

THE ROMANS MUST BE WARNED. YOU SWIM ACROSS THE RIVER AND DO THAT. I'LL TRY TO GET THAT WOMAN TO TRANSLATE MY WORDS CORRECTLY TO THE CHIEF!

RIGHT. I'LL GO AS SOON AS IT'S DARK. BUT YOU'LL BE STICKING YOUR HEAD RIGHT IN THE LION'S MOUTH.

GOD IS ANSWERING MY PRAYERS, ORPHEUS. THE CHIEF WILL HEAR THE TRUTH AND...

LISTEN! VOICES— THEY'RE COMING THIS WAY. WE'D BETTER HIDE!

WOMEN AND CHILDREN! WHAT ARE THEY DOING IN THE FOREST?

THEY'RE PROBABLY GOING TO THEIR SACRED GROVE TO COLLECT BRANCHES.

THEY'LL DECORATE THEIR ALTARS WITH GREENS AND PRAY TO THEIR PAGAN GODS FOR VICTORY. I'VE SEEN OTHER PAGANS DO THE SAME, BUT I NEVER KNEW IT TO HELP THEM!

EVERY CHILD IN THE VILLAGE MUST BE IN THAT GROUP. WHY ARE SOME CARRYING LIGHTED TORCHES IN THE DAYTIME?

TO KEEP EVIL SPIRITS OUT OF THE SACRED GROVE. WHEN THEY GET OUT OF SIGHT LET'S FOLLOW THEM!

AT THE SACRED GROVE ONE OF THE CHILDREN TRIPS ON A ROOT. THE TORCH FLIES OUT OF HER HAND AND LANDS ON A PILE OF DEAD LEAVES...

AND WITHIN SECONDS THE FLAMES RACE FROM TREE TO TREE, FANNED BY THE WIND!

TULLUS! IT'S A FOREST FIRE!

AND IT'S COMING FROM WHERE THE CHILDREN WERE GOING!

THE TWO RACE ALONG THE TRAIL AFTER THE CHILDREN AND SOON COME TO THE SACRED GROVE NOW NEARLY SURROUNDED BY FLAMES...

THEY'RE FROZEN IN FEAR. THEY'LL BE TRAPPED INSIDE THE CIRCLE OF FLAMES!

THERE'S THAT WOMAN WHO SPOKE TO US. THANK GOD! SHE CAN HELP US TELL THEM WHAT TO DO!

QUICKLY! TELL THEM TO BREAK OFF LENGTHS OF DRY REEDS—GET INTO THE LAKE—DUCK UNDER THE WATER AND BREATHE THROUGH THE REED STEMS!

FOR THE SHORT WHILE IT TAKES THE FLAMES TO ROAR ACROSS THE SACRED GROVE THE NEARLY TRAPPED GROUP DUCK BENEATH THE LAKE, BREATHING THROUGH THEIR REEDS.

THEN A HEAVY DOWNPOUR COOLS THE GROUND ENOUGH FOR THEM TO COME OUT OF THE WATER.

ALL NIGHT THEY HUDDLE TOGETHER, SHIVERING IN THE COLD RAIN. AT THE FIRST STREAK OF DAWN THEY HURRY BACK TO THE VILLAGE...TO FIND IT COMPLETELY DESTROYED BY THE FIRE! THEIR PARENTS GREET THEM WITH SHOUTS OF JOY.

THE CHILDREN! THE CHILDREN!

THEY ARE SAFE! OUR SADNESS IS TURNED TO JOY!

HOW IS IT YOU AND THESE ROMANS LEAD OUR CHILDREN OUT OF THE FOREST, WOMAN?

THEY SAVED THE CHILDREN, O CHIEF. WITHOUT THEIR HELP ALL WOULD HAVE SURELY DIED!

THE WOMAN SPEAKS BOLDLY TO THE CHIEF AS THE PEOPLE CROWD AROUND TO LISTEN...

MY MASTER, GERTH, HAS INTERPRETED THIS ROMAN'S WORDS FALSELY TO YOU. WHY, I DO NOT KNOW.

WHAT? YOU, A SLAVE, DARE ACCUSE YOUR MASTER?

WHILE MY MASTER TRADES AMBER FOR ROMAN GOLD AND PLOTS TO BECOME CHIEF WHEN YOU ARE SLAIN IN THE ATTACK ON THESE SAME ROMANS, THESE TWO MEN RISKED THEIR LIVES TO SAVE THE CHILDREN!

WHEN YOU SENT MESSENGERS TO CALL THE TRIBES TOGETHER FOR AN ATTACK ON ROME, I KNOW HE SENT OTHERS TELLING THEM TO LET YOU TEST THE ROMAN STRENGTH ALONE.

FOR A LONG WHILE THE CHIEF LISTENS AS THE WOMAN TELLS HOW GERTH HAS PLOTTED AGAINST HIM. THEN TULLUS IS ALLOWED TO EXPLAIN THE REAL KINGDOM OF GOD, AND CHRIST'S PROMISE OF SALVATION. THIS TIME HIS WORDS ARE CORRECTLY TRANSLATED.

YOUR WORDS RING TRUE, ROMAN! I UNDERSTAND MUCH THAT TROUBLED ME BEFORE. LET ME PONDER THEM. NOW, MY PEOPLE, RETURN TO YOUR TASKS OF REBUILDING YOUR HOMES!

DAYS GO BY AS THE VILLAGERS REBUILD THEIR HOMES. EVENINGS, WHEN WORK HAS STOPPED, TULLUS TELLS ABOUT JESUS TO ALL WHO WILL LISTEN. THE WOMAN, NOW FREED FROM SLAVERY BY THE CHIEF, TRANSLATES...

THE ROMAN GIVES ALL CREDIT FOR RESCUING OUR CHILDREN FROM THE FIRE TO HIS GOD.

AYE, MANY ARE TURNING FROM THE OLD GODS TO HIS. THE PRIESTS DO NOT LIKE IT.

AT THIS VERY MOMENT THE HEAD PRIEST IS TALKING TO HIS HELPERS...

THIS ROMAN IS TURNING THE PEOPLE AWAY FROM OUR GODS. HE MUST BE STOPPED!

HA! THAT WILL BE EASY, O HOLY ONE.

LEAVE IT TO US!

THAT NIGHT... TULLUS, ORPHEUS! WAKE UP—YOU MUST GET AWAY QUICKLY! THE PRIESTS ARE COMING TO SLAY YOU! HURRY!

HOW ABOUT YOU? THE PRIESTS KNOW YOU ARE A CHRISTIAN.

WON'T THEY SUSPECT THAT YOU HELPED US?

THEY CAN DO NOTHING TO ME. I TAKE CARE OF THE VILLAGE CHILDREN. I AM SAFE . . SOME DAY YOU WILL RETURN AND PREACH THE GOSPEL AGAIN TO THESE PEOPLE.

I DON'T LIKE RUNNING AWAY FROM THOSE WHO WERE JUST BEGINNING TO BELIEVE IN JESUS.

YOU'RE NOT RUNNING AWAY—JUST POSTPONING YOUR WORK UNTIL A BETTER TIME.

71

LANDING NEAR THE ROMAN FORT THEY ARE GRABBED BY THE SENTRY AND TAKEN TO THE COMMANDER...

YOU AGAIN? I TOLD YOU WHAT I'D DO IF YOU RETURNED!

WE CAME TO WARN YOU TO BE ON THE LOOKOUT FOR A SPY WHO...

HO—YOU MUST MEAN A VANDAL NAMED GERTH. WE CAUGHT HIM LAST NIGHT AFTER HE HAD LANDED WITH A LOAD OF AMBER. WE'VE BEEN WATCHING FOR HIM A LONG TIME. HE'LL SPY NO MORE.

SO THAT TAKES CARE OF GERTH, AND THE COMMANDER GAVE ME BACK MY HARP. I'LL SING A MARCHING SONG TO CHEER YOU UP ON OUR WAY TO LANI AND HER FATHER!

I STILL FEEL I SHOULD HAVE STAYED AND WORKED TO CONVERT MORE VANDALS TO CHRIST.

THE REUNION IS A HAPPY ONE.

YOU ARE SAFE! BUT WE KNEW GOD WAS PROTECTING YOU!

LANI!

ORPHEUS!

LATER THAT EVENING...

HOW CAN I ASK YOU TO MARRY ME WITH THIS BEAST LICKING MY CHEEK?

OH, HE KNEW WHAT YOU WERE GOING TO SAY AND HE'S SIMPLY TELLING YOU HE APPROVES!

DO NOT BE DOWNHEARTED, TULLUS. YOU HAVE PLANTED THE SEEDS OF CHRISTIANITY IN THE HEARTS OF MANY OF THE VANDALS THAT WILL BEAR RICH FRUIT. YOUR GOD IS PATIENT. YOU MUST BE, TOO.

THE END

72

TULLUS and the DRAGON SHIP

WITH A CLATTER OF HORSES' HOOVES THE ADVANCE GUARD OF A CELTIC TRADING PARTY DRAWS UP BEFORE THE GATES OF A VANDAL VILLAGE SHOUTING FOR ADMITTANCE.

THE GATES WHICH HAD BEEN SECURELY CLOSED WHEN THE CELTS HAD FIRST BEEN SIGHTED ARE QUICKLY OPENED. THE VILLAGERS JOYFULLY WELCOME THE TRADERS WHO COME IN PEACE.

TULLUS LOOKS ON WITH GREAT INTEREST.

PRAISE GOD! NOW I'LL HAVE A CHANCE TO TELL THESE TRIBESMEN FROM FAR AWAY ABOUT JESUS!

AS SOON AS THE MERCHANTS DISPLAY THEIR GOODS THE TRADING GOES ON BRISKLY.

THEN, AROUND THE CAMPFIRE THAT EVENING AFTER ALL HAVE FEASTED WELL, TULLUS TALKS TO THE VISITORS...

...AND THUS THE KINGDOM OF GOD IS REVEALED THROUGH JESUS CHRIST, OUR SAVIOR.

THE CELTS LISTEN TO TULLUS WITH INTEREST FOR THEY LOVE TO HEAR STORY-TELLING. BUT THEY FAIL TO UNDERSTAND HIS MESSAGE OF GOD'S LOVE.

THE LAD SPEAKS WELL. HE HAS A PLEASING VOICE.

AYE. IF HE TOLD OF BATTLES AND HUNTING I WOULD ENJOY LISTENING TO HIM MORE.

HE DOES NOT MENTION THE SPIRITS WHO LIVE IN OUR SACRED OAK TREES.

ONE OF THE CELTS, A BOY OF THE SAME AGE AS TULLUS, INTRODUCES HIMSELF TO TULLUS.

I AM CALLED ERIC. THEY TELL ME YOU ARE A ROMAN. I HAVE HEARD ROMANS ARE GREAT FIGHTERS YET YOU SPEAK ONLY OF KINDNESS BETWEEN MEN. ARE THE TALES I HAVE HEARD OF ROMAN BRAVERY FALSE?

NO, ERIC. ROMANS HAVE CONQUERED MOST OF THE WORLD WITH THEIR SWORDS. BUT IT TAKES GREATER COURAGE TO CONQUER MEN'S MINDS WITH WORDS OF TRUTH!

HO. I CANNOT BELIEVE THAT TALKING IS MORE COURAGEOUS THAN FIGHTING!

TULLUS SITS ON HIS STRAW-COVERED BED THAT NIGHT IN DEEP THOUGHT...

HELP ME O LORD. I'M NOT USING THE RIGHT WORDS TO REACH THESE PEOPLE. SHOW ME THE WAY, I PRAY YOU!

NEXT DAY TULLUS WATCHES THE VANDALS WHO CROWD INTO THE VILLAGE FROM FAR OFF MINES AND FIELDS AND FORESTS BRINGING GOODS TO TRADE, FOR NEWS OF THE ARRIVAL OF THE MERCHANTS HAS TRAVELED FAST.

MANY ARE FRIENDS WHOM TULLUS HAS WON TO CHRIST DURING HIS WANDERINGS AND HE IS GREETED WARMLY.

TULLUS! IT IS GOOD TO SEE YOU AGAIN! THANK GOD YOU ARE WELL.

OUR CHRISTIAN GROUP IS GROWING YOU'LL BE GLAD TO KNOW!

THEN ERIC, WHO IS HELPING HIS FATHER TRADE WEAPONS FOR SKINS, SEES TULLUS...

HO, ROMAN! COME, LET ME SHOW YOU A SHARP DAGGER THAT WOULD COME IN HANDY SHOULD YOU RUN OUT OF WORDS!

OR ARE YOU TOO FEARFUL TO HANDLE A WEAPON?

SILENCE, YOU! TULLUS HAS MORE COURAGE IN ONE FINGER THAN YOU HAVE IN YOUR WHOLE BODY!

I'LL SHOW YOU HOW MUCH...

STOP, STOP! DO NOT FIGHT OVER THE QUESTION OF COURAGE. GOD GIVES ALL MEN THE COURAGE TO DO WHAT IS RIGHT WHEN THEY PRAY TO HIM!

THE TRADING IS OVER IN A FEW DAYS. TULLUS BIDS GOOD-BY TO HIS FRIENDS AS THEY START OFF FOR THEIR DISTANT HOMES.

BEWARE OF THESE CELTS, TULLUS. THEY ARE AS WILD AND FIERCE AS THE DARK FORESTS THEY LIVE IN.

GOD IS MY PROTECTOR AS HE IS YOURS. DO NOT FEAR!

THAT NIGHT THE VILLAGE CHIEF ANNOUNCES...

TOMORROW WE INVITE ALL OUR CELTIC FRIENDS TO A WILD BOAR HUNT TO GIVE THEM FOOD FOR THEIR JOURNEY HOME.

ERIC CANNOT RESIST TAUNTING TULLUS...

DO YOU DARE FACE THE BOAR'S SHARP TUSKS, ROMAN? OR WILL YOU STAY WITH THE WOMEN AND CHILDREN SAFELY IN THE VILLAGE?

I WILL BE WITH THE HUNT, ERIC, AS A BEATER. YOU CELTS ARE GUESTS AND WILL BE THE HUNTERS.

EARLY NEXT MORNING THE HUNTERS START OUT FOLLOWING THE BEATERS WHO HAVE GONE AHEAD.

TULLUS AND THE MEN WHO ARE ACTING AS BEATERS FORM A LONG LINE, SHOUTING AND BANGING SHIELDS. THEIR OBJECT IS TO DRIVE THE GAME TOWARD THE HUNTERS. NOT FAR AWAY A HUGE BOAR, AROUSED BY THE STRANGE NOISE, LIFTS HIS UGLY HEAD WITH ITS SHARP, DEADLY TUSKS IN QUICK ANGER AT THIS DISTURBANCE.

78

ERIC AND A COMPANION HUNTER ARE IN THE DIRECT PATH OF THE FLEEING BOAR...

HERE HE COMES! IT'S YOUR FIRST HUNT, ERIC SO YOU MAY HAVE FIRST TRY AT THE PRIZE! DON'T MISS!

HA! I'LL HAVE THOSE TUSKS FOR A NECKLACE! WATCH...

BAH! YOU MISSED! YOU WERE TOO ANXIOUS AND CAST YOUR SPEAR TOO SOON!

NO! NO! I WOUNDED HIM! I SAW MY SPEAR GRAZE HIS SIDE!

WELL HE'S GONE NOW. I'LL TAKE THE NEXT BOAR AND SHOW YOU HOW TO DO IT RIGHT.

AND TELL EVERYONE WHAT A CLUMSY OAF I AM? NO! THIS BEAST IS MINE. I WOUNDED HIM. I'LL WIN HIS TUSKS!

DON'T BE FOOLISH. YOU'LL NEVER FIND HIM IN THOSE THICK REEDS. THERE'LL BE MORE BEASTS. WAIT!

NO! I WANT THIS ONE. HE HAD THE BIGGEST TUSKS I EVER SAW!

TULLUS AND SOME OTHER BEATERS COME RUNNING UP...

WHERE'S THE BOAR WE DROVE TO YOU?

HE GOT AWAY. ERIC THOUGHT HE'D WOUNDED HIM AND HAS GONE TO SEARCH IN THE REEDS.

IN THERE? AFTER A WOUNDED BOAR? THE BOAR MIGHT TURN ON HIM!

NO! THAT BOAR IS LEAGUES AWAY BY NOW! COME, LET'S GET BACK TO THE HUNT.

THE OTHERS CONTINUE THE HUNT—BUT NOT TULLUS.

I'M GOING IN JUST TO MAKE SURE ERIC'S ALL RIGHT...IF I CAN FIND HIM!

IN THE MEANTIME ERIC HAS REACHED AN OPEN AREA AFTER PUSHING HIS WAY THROUGH THICK REEDS FOR QUITE A DISTANCE.

DROPS OF BLOOD! HA, I DID WOUND THE BOAR! HE CAN'T BE FAR OFF!

SUDDENLY, AS SWIFTLY AND SILENTLY AS AN ARROW IN FLIGHT, THE BOAR SPEEDS OUT OF HIDING, KNOCKING ERIC TO THE GROUND WITH HIS UNEXPECTED RUSH!

THE MADDENED ANIMAL RUSHES AT ERIC...THEN TULLUS BURSTS INTO THE CLEARING!

ERIC! THANK YOU, GOD, YOU DIRECTED ME RIGHT TO HIM AND JUST IN TIME!

HE DRIVES OFF THE BOAR THEN RIPS UP HIS UNDERSHIRT TO MAKE BANDAGES.

YOU SAVED MY LIFE, ROMAN, DRIVING OFF THAT BOAR. AND WITH JUST A SMALL STICK! THAT TOOK REAL COURAGE! FORGIVE ME FOR TAUNTING YOU!

GOD GIVES COURAGE TO ALL WHO TRUST IN HIM, ERIC. NOW HOLD STILL SO I CAN BANDAGE YOUR WOUNDS. YOU'VE LOST A LOT OF BLOOD!

82

BY THE TIME THEY REACH THE VILLAGE THE OTHER HUNTERS HAVE RETURNED. A GREAT CELEBRATION IS GOING ON.

THEY HAVEN'T EVEN NOTICED THAT I WAS GONE! I COULD HAVE DIED FOR ALL THEY'D CARE!

UH, UH... DON'T JUDGE THEM. BESIDES IT'S JUST AS WELL...

ONE OF THE VANDALS MIGHT BOAST THAT THEY ARE BETTER HUNTERS THAN THE CELTS BECAUSE YOU DIDN'T BRING BACK YOUR BOAR AND A FIGHT WOULD START.

FOR THE NEXT FEW DAYS WHILE THE CELTS ARE GETTING READY TO RETURN HOME, ERIC STAYS UNNOTICED IN THE HUT HE SHARES WITH HIS FATHER.

WE'LL BE LEAVING TOMORROW BUT YOU'RE NOT READY FOR SUCH A HARD JOURNEY. I DON'T KNOW WHAT TO DO!

YOU GO ALONG WITH THE WAGON TRAIN, SIRE. TULLUS WANTS TO VISIT OUR COUNTRY. I'LL FOLLOW HIM AS SOON AS I'M ABLE TO RIDE AND CATCH UP TO YOU!

NEXT MORNING THE CELTS SAY GOOD-BY TO THEIR VANDAL HOSTS. WITH PROMISES TO COME BACK AGAIN WITH TRADE GOODS SOME DAY, THEY START OFF ON THE LONG JOURNEY HOME.

WE'VE GOT TO FIND MY PEOPLE AND WARN THEM BEFORE THOSE MURDEROUS SCYTHIANS POUNCE ON THEM!

I'LL PRAY THAT GOD WILL LET US GET THERE IN TIME!

TO AVOID BEING SEEN BY THE SCYTHIANS THEY KEEP TO THE CLIFFS WHERE ONE MISSTEP OF THEIR MOUNTS MEANS INSTANT DEATH ON THE CRUEL ROCKS BELOW!

HOURS LATER...

ERIC! THERE THEY ARE! THANK GOD!

AND NO SIGN OF THE SCYTHIANS! YOUR GOD HAS BEEN GOOD TO US, TULLUS!

THEY ARE WARMLY GREETED BY THE CELTS, PARTICULARLY BY ERIC'S FATHER.

WHEN TOLD OF THE SCYTHIAN RAIDERS, A COUNCIL OF WAR IS HELD...

THEY MUST BE HEADED FOR THE SMALL VILLAGE THAT LIES AROUND THAT BEND IN THE RIVER.

AND PASSED WITHOUT SEEING US.

THAT'S WHERE WE WERE GOING TO SPEND THE NIGHT!

86

THOSE WOLVES WILL DESTROY THE VILLAGE AND EVERY LIVING THING IN IT. WE'LL HAVE TO HIDE UNTIL THEY'VE DONE THEIR EVIL WORK AND GONE!

WE CAN'T LET THAT HAPPEN! WE MUST SAVE THOSE PEOPLE!

WE FEW CAN DO NOTHING. YOU SAW HOW MANY RAIDERS THERE WERE!

THERE **IS** A WAY! A MAN NAMED GIDEON DEFEATED A HUGE ARMY OF MIDIANITES ALTHOUGH HIS SMALL FORCE WAS GREATLY OUTNUMBERED. GOD WAS WITH HIM!

HO! BUT YOUR GOD DOES NOT KNOW US. WHY SHOULD HE COME TO OUR HELP?

GOD HELPS ALL WHO PUT THEIR TRUST IN HIM. DO NOT FEAR!

THAT'S TRUE, SIRE. TULLUS SAVED ME FROM THE WILD BOAR BECAUSE GOD WAS WITH HIM! I KNOW.

THE CELTS, ALWAYS EAGER FOR A BATTLE AGAINST THE SCYTHIANS, LISTEN AS TULLUS OUTLINES HIS PLAN.

WE SPLIT INTO TWO GROUPS. AT THE SIGNAL WE RUSH UPON THE RAIDERS FROM BOTH SIDES MAKING ALL THE NOISE WE CAN...

AND THEY'LL THINK WE'RE A GREAT HOST!

IT IS GOOD! WE'LL DO IT!

LET'S HOPE YOUR GOD IS WITH US!

MEANWHILE THE SCYTHIANS HAVE BEEN SPOTTED AND THE VILLAGE PREPARES FOR THEIR ATTACK.

MAN THE WALLS! THE SCYTHIANS COME!

CLOSE THE GATE! ANY LEFT OUTSIDE MUST HIDE IN THE FOREST!

HURRY— DON'T STOP THERE!

THE VILLAGERS LINE THEIR LOG STOCKADE...

THEY COME! THEY COME!

THE SCYTHIAN RAIDERS ARE WELL TRAINED IN WAYS TO ATTACK A WALLED VILLAGE. WHILE SOME SHOOT A BARRAGE OF ARROWS AT THE DEFENDERS, OTHERS RACE SWIFTLY TO THE GATE WITH BUNDLES OF FAGGOTS.

MORE HORSEMEN DASH UP AND THROW FLAMING TORCHES ON THE WOOD WHICH BURSTS INTO FLAMES THAT QUICKLY EAT INTO THE DRY, WOODEN GATE.

THE SMOKE BILLOWS SO HEAVILY IT BLINDS THE DEFENDERS ON THE WALL.

UNDER COVER OF THE SMOKE THE RAIDERS PREPARE TO SMASH DOWN THE FIRE-WEAKENED GATE WITH A HEAVY LOG BATTERING RAM SLUNG WITH ROPES BETWEEN TWO HORSEMEN.

THEN TULLUS AND HIS SMALL GROUP COME OUT OF THE FOREST.

THEY'VE FIRED THE GATE AND ARE MASSED TO RUSH IT! BLOW THE SIGNAL!

THE OTHER CELTS WAITING ON THE OPPOSITE SIDE OF THE VILLAGE HEAR THE RINGING NOTES...

THE SIGNAL— FORWARD!

AS THE CELTS RACE TO THE RESCUE THE PEOPLE WHO HAD HIDDEN THEMSELVES IN THE FOREST RUSH OUT TO JOIN IN THE BATTLE.

SEEING HORSEMEN AND OTHERS ON FOOT RUSHING TOWARD THEM FROM TWO SIDES, THE SCYTHIANS ARE COMPLETELY DEMORALIZED!

WE'RE TRAPPED BETWEEN TWO FORCES!

CALL OFF THE ATTACK! WE CAME TO RAID, NOT FIGHT SUCH A HORDE!

WITHOUT WAITING TO CHECK HOW SMALL WAS THE NUMBER OF CELTS CHARGING DOWN UPON THEM, THE SCYTHIANS GALLOPED AWAY.

WE'RE SAVED! BUT WHO ARE OUR RESCUERS?

WE'LL SOON KNOW! OPEN THE GATE AND PUT OUT THE FIRE SO OUR FRIENDS MAY BE WELCOMED!

WHEN THE CELTS RIDE UP TO THE STILL SMOLDERING GATE THE VILLAGERS WELCOME THEM IN AMAZEMENT...

HO! SO IT IS YOU TRADERS WHO CHASED THE SCYTHIANS AWAY!

JUST YOU FEW? THE WAY YOU RUSHED THEM YOU LOOKED LIKE AN ARMY!

THAT'S WHAT WE HOPED THE SCYTHIANS WOULD THINK AND THEY DID. THEY RAN AWAY BEFORE WE GOT CLOSE ENOUGH TO KILL ANY!

THE PLAN WAS THIS YOUNG ROMAN'S. THE BLOODLESS VICTORY IS DUE TO HIM!

GIVE THANKS TO GOD FOR SAVING YOU, NOT ME. ONLY THROUGH GOD'S GRACE CAN MEN OVERCOME EVIL. THOSE WHO BELIEVE IN HIM NEED NEVER FEAR!

THE VILLAGERS WONDER AT TULLUS' WORDS...

I WANT TO HEAR ABOUT THIS GOD THE LAD SPEAKS OF!

AYE! NONE OF OUR FOREST SPIRITS EVER SAVED A VILLAGE FROM SCYTHIAN RAIDERS!

THAT EVENING TULLUS talks to the people telling them about JESUS and his promise of salvation to all who follow him.

LATER some of the wagon train guards are sitting around their cooking fire talking about their remarkable victory over the fierce SCYTHIANS.

IT WAS MOST UNUSUAL FOR SCYTHIANS TO RUN OFF WITHOUT A BATTLE.

THE ROMAN SAYS OUR EASY VICTORY WAS BECAUSE OF HIS GOD.

AYE, AND SAYS NOTHING ABOUT OUR PART IN IT.

I GRANT YOU IT WAS HIS PLAN AND PERHAPS HIS GOD DID REVEAL IT TO HIM. BUT WHAT ABOUT US WHO RISKED OUR LIVES TO CARRY OUT THE PLAN?

THE SPIRITS THAT LIVE IN OUR SACRED OAKS PRAISE BRAVE MEN FOR THEIR COURAGE IN BATTLE AND LET THEIR DEEDS BE KNOWN FAR AND WIDE!

NO SAGAS OF OUR COURAGE WILL BE TOLD IN WARRIOR HALLS IF THIS STRANGER IS ALLOWED TO CONTINUE SAYING THE DEFEAT OF THE SCYTHIANS WAS DUE ONLY TO HIM AND HIS GOD!

I SAY THIS ROMAN MUST BE STILLED BEFORE WE REACH OUR HOMES!

BUT HIS BLOOD WOULD BE UPON OUR HANDS!

NOT IF HIS DEATH WAS BECAUSE OF AN ACCIDENT!

ERIC HAS OVERHEARD THE GUARDS TALKING AND WARNS TULLUS.

...SO BE ON YOUR GUARD AT ALL TIMES. THIS IS THEIR BIG CHANCE TO BRAG ABOUT THEIR HEROISM AGAINST GREAT ODDS!

AS SOON AS I CONVINCE THEM TO BELIEVE IN CHRIST THEY'LL KNOW WHAT TRUE HEROISM IS, ERIC!

92

NEXT DAY ALL PITCH IN TO BUILD RAFTS SO THEY CAN FLOAT DOWN TO THE MOUTH OF THE RIVER TO THEIR HOMES.

THE CELTS TRADE THEIR HORSES AND OXEN TO THE VILLAGERS FOR GOODS AND FOOD. NOW, THEIR RAFTS LOADED, THEY PUSH OFF WITH THE GRATEFUL PEOPLE'S HEARTY SHOUTS FOR A SAFE JOURNEY RINGING IN THEIR EARS.

FARTHER DOWN THE RIVER THEY REACH A STRETCH OF DANGEROUS RAPIDS. ONE OF THE RAFTS BUMPS INTO ANOTHER AND IS PUSHED OUT OF THE ONLY SAFE CHANNEL...

I CAN'T SWING US BACK! WE'RE HEADING RIGHT FOR THOSE ROCKS!

95

ONCE ASHORE, TULLUS RACES BACK UPSTREAM AS FAST AS HE CAN ALONG THE RUGGED BANK.

PLEASE GOD! HELP ME GET TO THEM IN TIME!

REACHING THE SCENE OF THE CRASH TULLUS FINDS THE THREE CELTS HANGING ONTO LOGS FROM THE WRECKED RAFT SPINNING 'ROUND AND 'ROUND IN A WHIRLPOOL FROM WHICH THEY CAN'T ESCAPE!

ONLY THE LOGS KEEP THEM FROM BEING SUCKED DOWN!

TAKING OFF HIS CLOTHES HE STRINGS THEM TO THE END OF A LONG BRANCH...

ONE BY ONE HE HAULS THE MEN ASHORE. THEN ERIC JOINS HIM AND BUILDS A FIRE TO WARM THE NEARLY EXHAUSTED GROUP AND DRY THEIR CLOTHES.

IF IT WASN'T FOR THIS CHRISTIAN WHOM YOU TRIED TO KILL YOU'D BE DEAD MEN BY NOW. I HOPE YOU REALIZE THAT!

FORGET THE PAST, ERIC. LET'S GIVE THANKS TO GOD THAT WE'RE ALL ALIVE NOW.

BY MORNING THEY ARE RESTED AND THEIR CLOTHES ARE DRY. ERIC LEADS THE WAY TO HIS BEACHED RAFT.

I'M WORRIED ABOUT THIS GROUP, TULLUS. THEY DON'T SEEM TO BE GRATFUL FOR BEING RESCUED!

THEY'RE PROBABLY STILL IN A STATE OF SHOCK, ERIC.

YOU DON'T KNOW THE CELTS, TULLUS. IF THESE MEN HAVE SWORN A BLOOD FEUD AGAINST YOU THEY'LL NEVER GIVE UP UNTIL YOU'RE DEAD! MAYBE WE SHOULD LEAVE THEM HERE AND GO HOME BY OURSELVES!

WE CAN'T DO THAT!

WE MUST FOLLOW CHRIST'S TEACHINGS, ERIC. AS LONG AS WE DO WHAT IS RIGHT WE NEED NOT FEAR. NEVER DOUBT GOD'S POWER TO OVERCOME EVIL!

REACHING THE RAFT, ERIC DOLES OUT A SMALL AMOUNT OF FOOD AND THEY PUSH OFF TO CONTINUE THEIR JOURNEY. ERIC WARNS THE RESCUED MEN...

WE'RE DANGEROUSLY OVERLOADED WITH YOU ON BOARD AND WE HAVEN'T MUCH FOOD. IF YOU HAVE ANY IDEAS ABOUT KILLING TULLUS AND ME, FORGET THEM!

I'D HAVE LEFT YOU TO DROWN AS YOU-TRIED TO DO TO US. BUT THIS ROMAN WORSHIPS A GOD WHO FORBIDS VENGEANCE AND INSISTED WE TAKE YOU ALONG. YOU OWE YOUR LIVES TO HIM.

FOR DAYS THEY GLIDE DOWN THE SWIFT-FLOWING RIVER WITHOUT ANY TROUBLE. THE THREE RESCUED CELTS TAKE THEIR TURN AT THE STEERING POLE. NONE COMPLAIN ABOUT THE SCARCITY OF FOOD AND ALL LISTEN QUIETLY WHEN TULLUS TELLS THEM ABOUT JESUS AND HIS WORKS.

THEN, AT LAST, THEY COME WITHIN SIGHT OF THEIR HOME!

THERE IT IS, TULLUS! WE MADE IT! I HOPE ALL THE OTHERS GOT HERE SAFELY, TOO!

I HAD NO IDEA IT WAS SO LARGE, ERIC! THIS ISN'T A VILLAGE, IT'S A CITY!

NEWS OF THEIR RETURN SPREADS RAPIDLY AND ALL THE TOWNSPEOPLE DROP WHATEVER THEY'RE DOING TO RUSH TO THE BEACH IN A HAPPY WELCOMING CROWD.

ERIC'S PARENTS GREET HIM JOYFULLY.

WE HAD MOURNED YOU TWO FOR LOST!

YOU ARE SAFE! AH, BUT YOU ARE SO THIN! I'LL SOON FATTEN YOU UP AGAIN!

THEY WELCOME TULLUS JUST AS WARMLY AND AFTER A HEARTY MEAL LISTEN TO THE TWO BOYS' EXPERIENCE UNTIL NEARLY DAWN.

HO, 'TIS LATE. TOMORROW YOU CAN TELL US MORE.

PARTICULARLY ABOUT THIS JESUS, TULLUS TALKS ABOUT.

WHILE IN ANOTHER PART OF TOWN THREE DRUID PRIESTS HUDDLE TOGETHER...

I QUESTIONED ALL EXCEPT ERIC AND THE ROMAN AND THAT'S WHAT THEY TOLD ME.

AND THEY SAID THAT ACCORDING TO THIS ROMAN IT WAS HIS CHRISTIAN GOD WHO SAVED THEM! HM-M-M, THIS COULD BE DANGEROUS TO US.

WE CAN'T LET THAT IDEA BE SPREAD AROUND LEST WE LOSE OUR POWER OVER THE PEOPLE!

IT IS NOW AROUND NOON. TWO OF THE DRUIDS ARE WALKING DOWN A NARROW STREET...

LOOK AT ALL THE PEOPLE BEFORE THAT HOUSE!

THAT'S WHERE ERIC AND HIS PARENTS LIVE. THE ROMAN WE SPOKE ABOUT MUST BE THERE. HE AND ERIC ARE GOOD FRIENDS!

THEY MOVE UP CLOSELY WHERE THEY CAN HEAR...

YOU HAVE COME TO WELCOME OUR BOY HOME? HOW GOOD OF YOU! COME IN, COME IN. WE'LL MAKE ROOM FOR ALL SOME WAY.

'TIS JUST A WELCOMING PARTY OF FRIENDS.

WAIT— LISTEN...

THIS IS ERIC'S FRIEND, TULLUS, A ROMAN. HE'LL TELL YOU ABOUT A GOD MUCH KINDER THAN OUR FOREST SPIRITS.

IT IS AS WE FEARED! HE'S DENYING THE EXISTENCE OF ALL GODS BUT HIS! IF THAT IDEA SHOULD SPREAD...

COME, WE MUST TELL THE HIGH PRIEST AT ONCE!

THEY HURRY TO THEIR SACRED GROVE WHERE THE HIGH PRIEST IS SITTING IN DEEP THOUGHT.

THE ROMAN HAS BEGUN HIS PREACHING ALREADY!

HOW CAN WE STOP HIM?

YOU SAY THE PEOPLE LISTENED TO HIM WITH GREAT INTEREST, EH?

AH! I HAVE IT! SUMMON EVERYONE TO BRING OFFERINGS TO OUR GODS HERE AT SUNRISE TWO DAYS HENCE IN GRATITUDE FOR OUR MEN'S SAFE RETURN.

THE PRIESTS ANNOUNCE THE COMING CEREMONY THROUGHOUT THE TOWN.

BAH! WHY DON'T THEY GET THEIR GODS TO HELP ME FINISH MY WORK!

IN THE MEANTIME THE PRIESTS BRAINWASH THE THREE MEN WHOM TULLUS SAVED...

...YOU HAVE ONLY THIS ROMAN'S WORD THAT IT WAS HIS GOD THAT SAVED YOU. ISN'T THAT SO?

AND WE HAVE HEARD HOW BRAVELY YOU AND THE OTHERS ATTACKED A LARGE FORCE OF SCYTHIANS. BUT THE ROMAN SAYS IT WAS HIS GOD, NOT YOU CELTS, WHO WON THE VICTORY!

THAT IS ALL TRUE!

ERIC HEARS RUMORS OF THE PRIEST'S DOINGS...

TULLUS, YOU MUST GET AWAY AT ONCE! THE DRUIDS PLAN TO KILL YOU!

I CAN'T, ERIC. MANY OF YOUR PEOPLE ARE TURNING TO CHRIST. I CAN'T DESERT THEM NOW!

THE DAY OF THE BIG CEREMONY DAWNS. TRUMPETERS LEAD THE WAY TO THE SACRED GROVE.

WHEN THE CHIEF DRUID ADDRESSES THE ASSEMBLED CROWD...

BRING FORTH YOUR OFFERINGS IN GRATITUDE TO THE SPIRITS THAT LIVE IN THE OAKS AND CAST THEM INTO THE SACRED STREAM. THUS MAY THE SPIRITS BE PLEASED AND...

WHY SHOULD WE PLEASE SPIRITS THAT DO NOT EXIST?

WE SHOULD PRAY TO THE ONE TRUE GOD INSTEAD!

THE CHIEF IS LIVID WITH RAGE AT THIS UNEXPECTED INTERRUPTION.

WHAT? WHO DARES DENY THE GODS THAT DWELL IN THIS SACRED GROVE? HA! THIS IS THAT ROMAN'S WORK!

I ACCUSE HIM OF BLASPHEMY AGAINST OUR ANCIENT GODS! PRIESTS—ARREST THE ROMAN! LET HIM STAND TRIAL FOR BECLOUDING OUR PEOPLE'S MINDS!

THE TOWNSPEOPLE ARE VIOLENTLY DIVIDED IN THEIR FEELINGS OVER TULLUS' GUILT OR INNOCENCE.

I WAS ONE OF THE TRADERS. IF IT HADN'T BEEN FOR THIS ROMAN'S GOD WE'D NEVER HAVE REACHED HOME SAFELY!

BEFORE YOU LEFT YOU GAVE OFFERINGS TO THE FOREST GODS. I SAW YOU!

SO DID I AND I THINK THEY PROTECTED YOU!

I HAVE HEARD THIS TULLUS SPEAK OF HIS GOD AND I WAS THRILLED. HIS IS A MUCH MORE KINDLY GOD THAN THOSE WE WERE BROUGHT UP TO WORSHIP.

THE ANCIENT GODS WERE GOOD ENOUGH FOR OUR ANCESTORS. THEY'RE GOOD ENOUGH FOR ME!

ERIC URGES TULLUS TO GET AWAY AT ONCE...

I'LL GO WITH YOU TULLUS. WE CAN BE MILES AWAY BEFORE THE PRIESTS ARREST YOU.

NO, ERIC, IF I RUN AWAY IT WILL BE AN ADMISSION OF GUILT.

TULLUS IS RIGHT...

IF HE CANNOT RELY ON HIS GOD TO HELP HIM IN THIS TIME OF NEED, WHO WOULD BELIEVE WHAT HE HAS BEEN PREACHING? HE MUST SEE THIS THROUGH!

THE PRIESTS DISCUSS THE SITUATION...

THIS ROMAN HAS INFLUENCED MORE PEOPLE THAN WE THOUGHT!

WE MUST BE CAREFUL HOW WE HANDLE HIM. CELTS ARE HOT-HEADED!

AYE. WE MUST NOT ARREST HIM AND DRAG HIM THROUGH THE STREETS LIKE AN ORDINARY CRIMINAL!

NO. HIS FOLLOWERS MIGHT SNATCH HIM FROM US. WE'D HAVE A RIOT ON OUR HANDS!

I KNOW WHAT WE'LL DO...

WE'LL ARREST HIM JUST BEFORE THE COCK CROWS IN THE MORNING. NO ONE'S IN THE STREETS AT THAT TIME. THEN WE'LL KEEP HIM OUT OF SIGHT UNTIL THE TRIAL!

WHEN TWO ARMED PRIESTS BURST INTO THE HOUSE...

COME WITH US, ROMAN!

NO, ERIC, NO! DON'T RESIST THEM. PUT UP YOUR SWORDS, PRIESTS. I COME!

FOR DAYS TULLUS IS KEPT HIDDEN BY THE PRIESTS. THEY ARE HOPING THE PEOPLE WILL LOSE SOME OF THEIR INTEREST IN HIM. BUT THOSE WHO HAVE TAKEN TULLUS' WORDS TO HEART AND TURNED TO CHRIST PUT UP SUCH A RACKET THAT THE CHIEF PRIEST IS FORCED TO NAME A DATE FOR THE TRIAL.

IT IS HELD IN AN OPEN FIELD NEAR THE WATERFRONT. THE WHOLE POPULATION ATTENDS...

BRING THE ACCUSED FORWARD. LET ANY WHO CAN WITNESS TO HIS OATH-WORTHINESS SPEAK UP NOW.

I SAY HE TELLS THE TRUTH.

I WILL WITNESS HE IS OATH-WORTHY.

HE DOES! HE DOES!

SO WILL I.

HE DOES NOT LIE!

SET HIM FREE!

HE IS OATH-WORTHY!

THE CELTS FIRMLY BELIEVED IN THE SOLEMNITY OF THE OATH. IF AN ACCUSED PERSON WAS CONSIDERED "OATH-WORTHY" HE WOULD BE FREED BY MERELY SWEARING HE TOLD THE TRUTH.

OTHERS COULD CLAIM HE WAS A TRUTHFUL PERSON AND HE COULD BE DEEMED OATH-WORTHY.

BUT ALTHOUGH MANY SWORE TULLUS WAS OATH-WORTHY, THE DRUIDS HAD NO INTENTION OF LETTING HIM OFF SO EASILY.

THE CHIEF DRUID ANNOUNCED NOT ENOUGH WITNESSES HAD SPOKEN UP IN FAVOR OF TULLUS. HE DEMANDED THAT TULLUS' GUILT OR INNOCENCE OF THE ACCUSATION BE DETERMINED BY EITHER TRIAL BY BATTLE OR TRIAL BY ORDEAL!

AT THIS ANNOUNCEMENT ERIC STEPS UP BESIDE TULLUS...

LET IT BE TRIAL BY BATTLE. I WILL BE HIS CHAMPION!

NO, ERIC, I WILL NOT LET YOU RISK YOUR LIFE THAT WAY.

I DEMAND TRIAL BY ORDEAL!

THE CROWD GASPS. THIS IS THE MOST TERRIBLE TRIAL OF ALL. NO ONE HAS EVER SURVIVED IT!

106

AT SUNSET THE TRUMPETERS SUMMON ALL THE VILLAGERS TO WITNESS THE TRIAL BY ORDEAL..

EVERYONE FOLLOWS TO THE OPEN FIELD DOWN NEAR THE BEACH. A COUPLE OF BOYS CLIMB TO THE THATCHED ROOF OF A NEARBY HOUSE FOR A BETTER VIEW.

THIS IS BETTER THAN TRYING TO PUSH THROUGH THAT CROWD!

IF WE DON'T GET A BEATING FOR CLIMBING UP HERE!

THE CHIEF DRUID SCRATCHES A LARGE CIRCLE IN THE DIRT. HE AND OTHER DRUIDS STAND IN THE CENTER. HE ANNOUNCES TO THE CROWD...

THE ACCUSED MAY WRAP LEAVES AROUND HIS HANDS. THEN HE MUST CARRY THE IRON BALL AROUND THE MAGIC CIRCLE. IF HIS HANDS ARE BURNED EVEN SLIGHTLY HE IS PROVED GUILTY AS CHARGED AND WILL BE PUT TO DEATH.

HE CONTINUES WITH A LONG SPEECH DENOUNCING TULLUS. THEN, JUST AS THE FULL MOON PEEPS OVER THE EASTERN HILLS THE TRUMPETS ARE BLOWN...

AND TWO DRUIDS, CARRYING A BRAZIER OF GLOWING COALS, COME QUICKLY TO THE FIELD.

THEY PLACE IT BEFORE THE CHIEF DRUID. A GROAN OF HORROR SWEEPS OVER THE CROWD SEEING THE TERRIBLE IRON BALL THAT TULLUS IS DOOMED TO CARRY SHIMMERING WITH HEAT!

ALL EYES ARE FOCUSED ON THE BRAZIER. SUDDENLY, ONE OF THE BOYS ON THE ROOFTOP SCREAMS...

A DRAGON SHIP! A DRAGON SHIP!

UNNOTICED BY ANYONE A VIKING SHIP HAD SNEAKED INTO THE HARBOR. THE FIERCE SEA PIRATES ARE TUMBLING ASHORE AND RACING UP THE SLOPE BY THE TIME THE BOY'S WARNING SHRIEK IS HEARD. THE STUNNED CELTS STAND FROZEN IN SHOCK FOR A FEW MINUTES...

THEN THEY RUSH IN PANIC FROM THE FIELD, SOME TO GRAB WEAPONS TO DEFEND THEIR VILLAGE, OTHERS INTENT ONLY IN GETTING AWAY TO HIDE FROM THESE MERCILESS INVADERS!

ERIC WAS JUST STARTING TO WRAP LEAVES AROUND TULLUS' HANDS WHEN THE WARNING WAS SHOUTED...

SEA WOLVES FROM THE NORTH! THEY'VE CAUGHT US UNAWARES!

THERE'S BUT ONE CHANCE TO SAVE THE VILLAGE!

THEY'RE SURE TO CALL OFF THEIR ATTACK WHEN THEY SEE THEIR SHIP ON FIRE!

IF WE CAN GET TO IT WITHOUT BEING CAUGHT!

TULLUS AND ERIC ACT SO SWIFTLY THE VIKINGS ARE JUST ENTERING THE VILLAGE WHEN FLAMES BEGIN TO SHOOT UP FROM THEIR BEACHED SHIP!

THE SHIP IS AFIRE! FORM A REAR GUARD—RETURN TO THE BEACH! WITHOUT OUR SHIP WE ARE LOST!

THE BRAVEST OF THE VILLAGERS, WHO RUSHED TO ARM THEMSELVES, NOW ADVANCE ON THE DREADED VIKINGS...

THEY ARE FLEEING! THEIR SHIP IS AFIRE! ATTACK! ATTACK!

SOME OF THE VIKINGS FORM A SHIELD-LINE WHILE OTHERS TRY TO QUENCH THE FIRE. THE VILLAGERS PAUSE MOMENTARILY BEFORE CHARGING AGAINST THIS LINE OF DETERMINED WARRIORS. ONLY THE CRACKLING FLAMES CAN BE HEARD AS THE TWO GROUPS FACE EACH OTHER.

TULLUS LEAPS BETWEEN THE TWO FORCES...

STOP! IN THE NAME OF JESUS CHRIST I CALL UPON BOTH SIDES TO DROP THEIR WEAPONS!

NEITHER THE CELTS NOR THE VIKINGS HAVE EVER HEARD SUCH A COMMAND BEFORE.
THEY ALL STARE AT TULLUS IN AMAZE-MENT AS HE CONTINUES...

THE ORDEAL THAT WAS MEANT TO KILL ME HAS INSTEAD SAVED THE VILLAGE BECAUSE THE ONE TRUE GOD SO WILLED IT. HIS MERCY IS NOT TO BE TURNED INTO A BLOOD-FEUD. KILLING EACH OTHER NOW WILL GAIN NOTHING. LET EACH SIDE CHOOSE A SPOKESMAN TO TALK WITH ME.

AWED BY HIS FORCEFUL SINCERITY THE VIKING CHIEF AND THE VILLAGE HEADMAN DROP THEIR WEAPONS AND WALK UP TO TULLUS...

I WILL LISTEN TO YOU, STRANGER, BUT NOT BECAUSE I OR MY MEN FEAR DEATH!

I WILL LISTEN BECAUSE I HAVE HEARD YOU SPEAK OF YOUR GOD AND I BELIEVE YOU ARE HONEST AND JUST!

110

AFTER A LONG CONFERENCE...

IT IS AGREED. OUR PEOPLE PROMISE NEVER TO ATTACK THIS COUNTRY-SIDE OR ITS VILLAGES AGAIN.

AND YOU MAY STAY IN PEACE TO REBUILD YOUR SHIP. MAY OUR OATHS NEVER BE BROKEN!

THE VILLAGERS AND THE VIKINGS, TOO, ARE HAPPY OVER THE PEACEFUL SETTLEMENT. SOME OF THE VIKINGS FIND TIME WHILE REBUILDING THEIR BURNED SHIP TO MINGLE WITH SOME OF THE VILLAGE PEOPLE...

IN ALL MY TRAVELS I HAVE NEVER SEEN A GIRL SO FAIR AS YOU!

OH—I'M SURE YOU SAY THAT TO EVERY GIRL!

AND WHEN TULLUS HOLDS HIS REGULAR PRAYER MEETINGS THE ATTENDANCE KEEPS GROWING...

...AND WHEN PETER DREW HIS SWORD AND CUT ONE OF THE SOLDIERS, JESUS TOLD HIM TO PUT HIS SWORD DOWN. THEN JESUS HEALED THE MAN'S WOUND...

WHICH DISTURBS THE DRUIDS, BUT THERE'S NOTHING THEY DARE DO TO PREVENT IT.

OUR FOLLOWERS GET FEWER ALL THE TIME!

AYE! THE FOREST SPIRITS HAVE BEEN CONQUERED BY THIS ROMAN'S GOD! OUR HOLD OVER THE PEOPLE IS LOST!

WHEN THE REBUILT DRAGON SHIP SAILS OFF IT IS MINUS MANY OF ITS CREW...THOSE WHO HAVE CHOSEN WIVES AMONG THE CELTS AND HAVE GIVEN UP SEA-ROVING TO BECOME PEACEFUL VILLAGERS.

ARE YOU SURE YOU WILL NEVER FORGET YOUR DECISION?

I'M SURE! I HAVE LEARNED A BETTER WAY OF LIFE THAN I EVER KNEW BEFORE.

JUST THINK, TULLUS. I WOULD NEVER HAVE KNOWN ABOUT JESUS IF YOU HADN'T SAVED ME FROM THAT WILD BOAR!

IT IS JESUS WHO SAVES, ERIC. ALL THAT WE WHO BELIEVE IN HIM CAN DO IS POINT THE WAY TO SALVATION!

THE END

111